iPhone

— FOR —

SENIORS

FROM GRAY HAIR TO TECH FLAIR!

An Easy and Empowering Guide to
Independence, Security, and Staying Connected
That Will Leave You Chuckling at Tech Challenges

SAGE DEVICE INSIGHTS

ACKNOWLEDGMENTS

First and foremost, I express my profound gratitude to the Almighty for the guidance and strength on this journey.

This book is a testament to the collective effort of many incredible individuals. Thank you for turning this dream into reality.

I am immensely grateful to Rocío Martín Osuna for her creative vision and artistic talent in designing the book cover.

I want to thank Katrina Johanson for her invaluable advice and insights that have contributed significantly to this project, Publishing Services for their professionalism, attention to detail, and commitment to quality, and the entire team at Publishing.com for their exceptional support and guidance.

I am profoundly grateful to my friends and family for being generous with their time and providing feedback, and to you, the reader, your support and engagement are cherished.

Contents

INTRODUCTION

Navigating the world of smartphones, especially for seniors or late adopters of technology, can be daunting. I've witnessed this firsthand through my own grandmother's experience with her new iPhone. She was thrilled when she received it as a gift from her grandson but was quickly overwhelmed by the myriad of symbols and unfamiliar terms that greeted her on the screen.

In an attempt to ease her into the phone's features, I thought teaching her to take a simple selfie would be a good start. Little did I expect that instead of capturing her face, she managed to snap a photo of her ear! We both shared a hearty laugh, but it taught me a valuable lesson: Teaching seniors to use an iPhone isn't just about explaining technical jargon. It's equally about instilling confidence and comfort in using technology.

Welcome to a personalized journey through the incredible world of iPhone technology designed specifically for seniors or those less familiar with tech. We'll dive into all the **features of the iPhone X and beyond**. This guide isn't your typical iPhone manual; it's your companion, guiding you through every step with simplicity and clarity. I've tailored this guide to ensure that using your iPhone becomes a delightful experience rather than a daunting challenge.

This book is your key to unlocking the potential of your iPhone for communication, entertainment, and maintaining connections with family and friends. It stands out because it's crafted for those not well-versed in technology. Expect a step-by-step approach, accompanied by large print, crystal-clear descriptions, and practical tips for everyday use. Moreover, sprinkled throughout are anecdotes and humor to keep you engaged and motivated.

Forget about struggling through the iPhone maze alone. This guide is here to hold your hand through every feature and function. With an easy-to-read font size and clear visuals, there's no strain on your eyes or need for magnification.

Gone are the days of complex technical terms causing confusion. We've replaced the jargon with simple language, making iPhone concepts crystal clear. You'll not only understand what each term means but also how to seamlessly use it in your day-to-day interactions with your iPhone.

We'll cover the basics and delve a bit deeper:

1. Getting started: This section kickstarts your iPhone journey, guiding you through setup, and basic functions, and introducing you to features like Siri.

2. Communicating: Learn to make calls, send texts, utilize FaceTime for video calls, and manage your contacts. Plus, explore social media apps to stay connected.

3. Having fun: Discover the entertaining side of your iPhone, from taking and editing photos to enjoying music, videos, and books.

4. Exploring further: Dive into advanced features such as using the App Store, browsing the web via Safari, navigating with Maps, and monitoring health with Health. Manage your daily life using apps like Calendar, Notes, Clock, Calculator, and Weather.

By the end of this journey, you'll feel confident and empowered in wielding your iPhone. You'll effortlessly communicate, entertain yourself, and explore various functionalities, staying connected with your loved ones and the wider world. Remember, there's no rulebook for using your iPhone; it's about finding your unique way, and that's always the best way for you.

You set the pace here. Skip what doesn't pique your interest and dive into what excites you. The more you engage with your iPhone, the more comfortable and confident you'll become. So, grab your iPhone, and let's embark on this fun, easy, rewarding, and enjoyable journey together!

CHAPTER 1

First Steps with Your New Companion

An iPod, a phone, an internet mobile communicator… these are NOT three separate devices! And we are calling it the iPhone! Today Apple is going to reinvent the phone. And here it is.
— **Steve Jobs**

On January 9, 2007, Steve Jobs, the visionary co-founder and CEO of Apple, took the stage and introduced the world to the iPhone. This groundbreaking moment marked a paradigm shift in the realm of mobile technology. Jobs unveiled not just a phone, but a device that would revolutionize communication, entertainment, and connectivity forever.

The inaugural iPhone ingeniously amalgamated the functions of a music player, a phone, and an internet device into a sleek, all-in-one package. It wasn't merely a communication tool; it was a gateway to a new era. This device redefined the possibilities of what a phone could be and reshaped how people interacted, entertained themselves, and stayed connected.

With each subsequent generation, the iPhone has undergone remarkable evolution and enhancement, continually offering more features, capabilities, and advantages. Today's iPhone is not just a communication device; it's a versatile companion that empowers you to:

- Make calls, send texts, and conduct video calls

- Explore the internet, access emails, and engage in social media

- Capture stunning photos and videos using high-resolution cameras

- Enjoy a vast library of music, podcasts, and audiobooks

- Watch a plethora of shows and movies

- Read books and magazines with customizable font sizes and brightness

- Play games and use a wide array of apps

- Monitor health and fitness metrics

- Navigate seamlessly with maps

- Make convenient payments for goods and services

The iPhone has transcended its initial role to become an integral part of daily life. It has not only simplified tasks but also expanded our horizons, offering us new avenues to explore and enjoy. It embodies convenience, entertainment, and efficiency.

Before diving into this world of possibilities, it's essential to set up and acquaint yourself with the basics of your iPhone. This chapter acts as your guide, ensuring that by the end, you'll feel more at ease and confident in setting up and navigating your iPhone, paving the way for an enriching, and fulfilling iPhone experience.

Unboxing Your iPhone: More Than Just a Phone

Unboxing your new iPhone is an exciting first step into the world of Apple's technology. The packaging Apple provides is not only sleek but also informative, giving you a comprehensive overview of what you'll find inside.

Upon opening the box, you'll discover a neatly arranged set of essentials, including:

1. Your iPhone, wrapped in its protective covering and ready to be activated.

2. An essential Lightning or USB-C charging cable.

3. A wall-plug that pairs with the charging cable to connect your iPhone to a power outlet for charging.

4. A tiny metallic pin-shaped SIM Card tool, used to eject the SIM card tray to insert or change the SIM card in your iPhone.

5. A quick guide that provides essential tips for setting up and using your iPhone, and a warranty card that outlines details about your iPhone's warranty and provides contact information for Apple support.

It's crucial to keep the original box and its contents in a safe place. They might come in handy in various scenarios such as identifying your iPhone model and serial number, facilitating returns or exchanges, or utilizing the charging cable, wall plug, and SIM card tool. Moreover, retaining the original packaging can enhance the appeal of your iPhone if you ever decide to sell or gift it to someone else.

This initial unboxing experience not only sets the stage for your iPhone setup but also emphasizes the importance of safeguarding the box and its contents for future use.

Powering Up: The First Hello

Turning on your iPhone for the first time is an exciting start to your journey with this amazing device. Before you dive in, there are a few steps to get things rolling.

1. **Power button**

   The power button is a long, slim button on the right side of your iPhone. Press and hold it until you see the Apple logo on the screen, indicating your iPhone is turning on.

2. "Hello"

When your iPhone starts up, it'll greet you with a "Hello" message in different languages. Swipe up from the bottom of the screen to begin. Choose your language and region by tapping your preferences and then the blue arrow.

3. Wi-Fi

Connect to a Wi-Fi network to access the internet. Tap your Wi-Fi network's name, enter the password if needed, and tap "Join." If Wi-Fi isn't available, tap "Use Cellular Connection." Remember, using cellular data might lead to charges.

4. Apple ID

This is your personal key to Apple services. Sign in with your existing Apple ID or create a new one by following the prompts. This ID is crucial for updates, support, and accessing Apple's ecosystem.

5. Face ID

If your iPhone supports it, you can set up Face ID to unlock your device and use apps securely. You can do this now or later through the Settings app. Follow the on-screen instructions to set it up.

6. Accessibility options

Customize features like text size and voiceover during setup or later in the Settings app. These options can help if you have vision, hearing, or motor challenges.

Remember, your Apple ID and Face ID are essential for a smooth experience with your iPhone. Now that you've said "Hello" to your iPhone, get ready to explore more of its incredible features!

Customizing Accessibility Features

Your iPhone offers ways to make it more accessible, especially if you have vision, hearing, or motor challenges.

Let's check out a few of these helpful features:

Note: **These features will be covered in more detail in Chapter 8**

1. Zoom

Enlarge your screen by tapping the button next to Zoom and adjusting the zoom level. You can activate it with a double tap using three fingers or by using the Zoom controller.

2. Display and text size

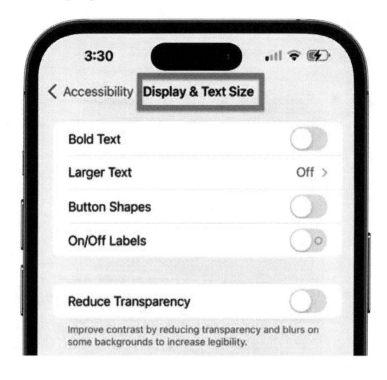

This feature lets you adjust brightness, text size, boldness, and contrast for better readability. You can turn on Smart Invert to change display colors except for images, Auto-Brightness for adjusting screen brightness automatically, or Reduce White Point for less intense colors.

3. Voiceover

Get spoken descriptions of what's on your screen with VoiceOver. Tap the button next to it to activate it, then adjust the speaking rate and volume. Tap the screen to hear what's under your finger and use specific gestures to navigate.

Once you've set these features to your preference, tap the blue arrow to continue. If you want to skip this setup, tap "Skip Accessibility" in the top right corner. Remember, you can always adjust these settings later in the Settings ⚙ app under Accessibility. Plus, use the Accessibility Shortcut by triple-clicking the power button for quick access to your favorite accessibility feature.

Charging Your iPhone: Keeping the Power Flowing

Keeping your iPhone charged is crucial for staying connected and enjoying its features throughout the day. Let's explore two ways to charge it: using a cable or opting for wireless charging.

The traditional method involves using the USB cable included in your iPhone box:

Step one: Plug the USB-C end of the cable into a USB-C port on your computer or a separate power adapter. If using an adapter, plug it into a wall outlet.

Step two: Connect the Lightning end of the cable to your iPhone's charging port located at the bottom. Upon connection, you'll hear a chime and a lightning bolt icon appears next to the battery icon, indicating charging.

Keep your iPhone connected until it reaches full charge. Check the battery icon on your screen; it turns green at 100%. You can also view the estimated remaining charging time by tapping the battery icon.

For wireless charging, follow these steps:

1. Select a compatible charger

    Not all wireless chargers work with every iPhone model. Look for Qi-certified wireless chargers or specifically designed MagSafe chargers, available at Apple Stores or other retailers.

2. Connect the charger

    Plug the wireless charger into a power source, like a wall outlet or computer, using the cable provided with the charger. Ensure you're using the correct cable and power adapter for optimal charging.

3. Place your iPhone

    Position your iPhone on the wireless charger, ensuring proper alignment. Once placed correctly, you'll hear a sound and see a lightning bolt icon near the battery icon on your iPhone's screen, indicating wireless charging.

Keep your iPhone on the charger until it reaches a full charge. Monitor the battery icon: When it turns green and displays 100%, your iPhone is fully charged. You can also check the estimated remaining charging time by tapping the battery icon.

Your iPhone's "Optimized Charging" feature intelligently manages your battery's health by learning your charging habits.

How it works:

- Charges up to 80%, pausing before your usual waking time to prevent long-term damage from constant full charges, safeguarding your battery from prolonged full charges.

To optimize battery life:

- Check the charging indicator for status and unplug when fully charged.

- Charging times vary based on factors like usage and temperature.

- Usage while charging is fine but may slow charging speed.

- Overnight charging may be unnecessary with Optimized Charging.

- Monitor battery health in Settings ⚙ > Battery > Battery Health.

Optimized Charging streamlines your charging routine, ensuring convenience and longevity for your iPhone's battery.

Recognizing Your iPhone's Buttons and Features: An External Tour

To maximize your iPhone's functionality, familiarize yourself with its external features, including buttons and switches. These components play crucial roles in controlling and interacting with your device

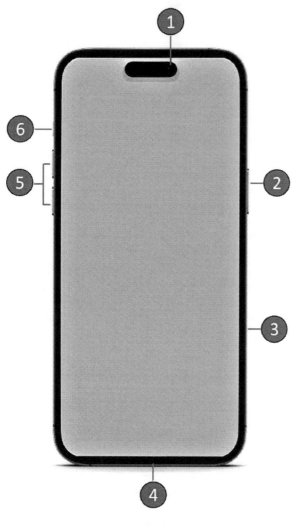

1. Front facing cameras.

2. Power Button to lock and turn off your phone.

3. Sim Tray for physical SIMs Note: Newer phones have eSIMs

4. A lightning cable connector to charge the phone and connect to devices.

5. Volume buttons

6. Mute/Unmute button.

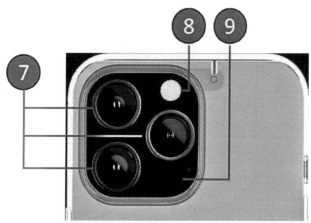

7,8, 9 – Back cameras

Note: The back cameras may look different for each iPhone model

1. The power button

   Functions: This long, thin button on the right side of your iPhone serves multiple purposes.

   Power On/Off: Hold it to turn your iPhone on/off.

   Lock/Unlock: Tap to lock or unlock your iPhone.

   Wake/Sleep: Single press to wake or sleep your device.

   Screenshot: Simultaneously press the volume up button to capture your screen.

   Siri Activation: Long press to activate Siri, your voice assistant.

   Emergency SOS: Press and hold to call emergency services or notify emergency contacts.

2. The volume buttons

   Utility: These buttons on the left side allow you to:

   Adjust Volume: Control media or ringer volume depending on your activity.

   Mute/Unmute: Silence ringer/alert sounds using the volume down button or the mute switch above.

3. The mute switch

   Purpose: Located above the volume buttons, this switch toggles your iPhone's sound on/off, affecting ringer/alert sounds while leaving media sounds unchanged.

Understanding these buttons and features empowers you to navigate and control your iPhone efficiently.

Understanding the SIM Card: Your Link to the World

Your iPhone's SIM card is your gateway to the cellular network, enabling calls, texts, and data usage.

Here's what you need to know about managing it:

Activation and insertion:

- Ensure compatibility and activation of your SIM card, whether provided by your carrier or transferred from a previous device.

- Use a SIM card tool or paper clip to gently access the slot on the right side of your iPhone, inserting the card with the gold contacts facing down and aligned with the tray's notch. Slide it securely back in.

SIM Card Care:

- Handle the SIM card delicately, avoiding contact with the gold contacts and exposure to moisture, bending, extreme temperatures, or magnets.

- In case of loss, damage, or theft, promptly contact your carrier for a replacement.

Newer models in the US (such as iPhone 15, 14, 13, 12, 11, and XS) feature an embedded SIM (eSIM) for multiple plans or carriers without a physical card. Refer to carrier instructions or Apple's resources for eSIM setup.

Understanding these SIM card fundamentals optimizes your iPhone's connectivity, ensuring seamless communication and utilization of its capabilities.

Using the User Guide: An Often Overlooked Helper

Your iPhone's user guide is a treasure trove of knowledge, from the basics to advanced features.

1. Unearthing invaluable insights

   Comprehensive knowledge: It covers setup, operation, customization, troubleshooting, and more, offering a deep dive into your iPhone's capabilities.

   Tips and hidden gems: Discover lesser-known features, tips, and tricks that enhance your iPhone experience.

   Problem-solving aid: It's a go-to resource for resolving issues or seeking guidance when navigating your iPhone.

2. Access and convenience

   Ease of understanding: Crafted in simple language with helpful visuals for easy comprehension.

   Organized information: Chapters, sections, a table of contents, an index, and a search function aid in locating specific information.

   Digital accessibility: Available online, downloadable in various formats for offline access, and compatible across devices.

3. Keeping up-to-date

   Regular updates: Consistently updated to match the latest iPhone enhancements and software changes.

   Accessible updates: Easily accessible via Apple's website or iBooks app, ensuring you have the latest information at your fingertips.

4. Essential companion

   Underappreciated resource: Often overlooked but serves as a reliable problem solver and educator, saving time and effort.

   Cost and time saver: Reduces the need for unnecessary support calls or store visits, empowering self-sufficiency.

As you delve deeper into your iPhone journey, Chapter Two awaits, offering insights into your device's interface. This chapter elucidates your iPhone's layout, icon management, and how to navigate using gestures, buttons, and menus. It's a roadmap to unlocking the intuitive and user-friendly nature of your iPhone.

CHAPTER 2

Cracking the Code - Understanding Your iPhone's Interface

Anything can change because the smartphone revolution is still in the early stages.
— **Tim Cook**

Your iPhone is more than just a device; it's an intricate and versatile tool that adapts to your preferences. Mastering its interface is essential to harness its full potential. In this chapter, we'll immerse ourselves in the elements that define your iPhone's interaction.

1. Understanding the interface: Delve into the screen, buttons, gestures, and menus that shape your iPhone experience. Familiarize yourself with the intuitive design, crafted to accommodate various needs and preferences.

2. Home screen navigation: Explore the gateway to your iPhone's capabilities — the Home screen. Learn to navigate seamlessly between apps, organize them, and understand how to access and utilize your iPhone's core functions.

3. Control center unveiled: Unlock the secrets of the Control Center, a treasure trove granting quick access to essential settings and functions. Discover how to tweak and control various aspects of your device with a simple swipe.

4. Customizing your settings: Take charge of your iPhone's settings, tailoring them to your unique requirements. Uncover shortcuts, insights, and personalized tweaks that enhance your iPhone experience, making it a more intuitive and friendly companion.

This chapter serves as your guide, offering the skills and knowledge necessary to traverse your iPhone's interface effortlessly. By understanding its intricacies and customization options, you'll transform your iPhone into a more approachable and accommodating device, poised to meet your needs seamlessly. Let's embark on this journey of discovery and empowerment together!

Getting Acquainted With Your Home Screen: Your New Best Friend

Your Home screen is like the face of your iPhone—a vibrant canvas that welcomes you upon unlocking the device. It's a hub where you access all your apps, from the built-in essentials to those you've added from the App Store. This screen offers more than just apps; it provides quick glimpses of the time, date, battery life, and other key indicators.

But it's not just a single screen; it's a series of pages you can swipe through, each accommodating up to 24 app icons neatly arranged in a grid, with a layout of four rows and six columns per page. And you're not limited to just apps; you can also include widgets—small windows displaying app information or shortcuts—tailored to your needs.

Accessing your Home screen is easy: A simple swipe up from the bottom edge of the screen does the trick, seamlessly taking you back to your Home screen from any point. Another swipe up lands you right on the initial page of your Home screen.

To transition between Home screens, you can opt for one of these methods.

- Execute a horizontal swipe, left or right, on the screen to navigate to the preceding or subsequent page of your Home screen.

- Alternatively, tap the dots situated at the bottom of the screen to leap to a specific page on your Home screen. The highlighted dot indicates the page you currently occupy.

Let's look at some of the basic apps you'll find on your phone's home screen.

Safari	
	**What it does:** Safari is your window to the internet. You can explore websites and change how it works. **Easy changes:** You can make it start on a specific webpage, choose your favorite search engine, and keep your browsing private.
Calendar	
	**What it's for:** Calendar helps you organize your time. You can make plans and remember important dates. **What you can do:** Add events like meetings or birthdays and set reminders for things you shouldn't forget.

Photos

For your pictures and videos: Photos keeps all your photos and videos tidy.

What you can do: Organize your pictures in groups and make simple changes like cropping or adding filters.

Camera

For taking pictures and videos: The camera helps you capture moments.

What you can do: Take different kinds of photos like close-ups or wide shots, and record videos in slow motion or fast-forward.

Maps

Finding your way: Maps help you get directions and find places.

What you can do: Search for places and save spots you want to remember.

Weather

What to expect outside: Weather tells you what it's like outdoors now and later.

What you can see: Current weather details and forecasts for upcoming days.

Clock

Alarm and time features: The clock helps you wake up and track time.

What it offers: Set alarms, check different time zones, use a stopwatch or timer.

News

For staying updated: News brings stories from different sources.

What you can do: Read news stories and save them for later, share them with friends.

Music

Your music hub: Music lets you listen to songs on your phone and find more.

What it does: Play your music and make playlists for different moods or activities.

Settings

The control center: Settings is where you can adjust how your phone works.

What you control: Change things like Wi-Fi, security, and how your screen looks.

Magnifier

Helps you see better: Magnifier makes things easier to read or see.

What it does: Zoom in on small text or objects and use light for better visibility.

Dock Customization

Step 1

Alpharetta	⌁
New York	⚓
Add	+
Edit Home Screen	
Remove App	⊖

Quick access panel: The Dock holds your favorite apps for quick use.

How to change it: Tap and hold an app, then move it to the Dock area.

Step 2

Step 3

Notification Center

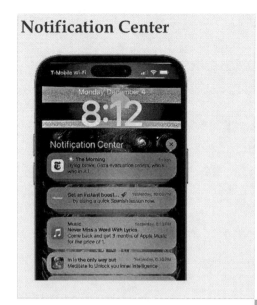

Updates in one place: The Notification Center shows messages and alerts.

How to get there: Swipe down from the top of your screen.

Control your alerts: Choose which apps can send you messages and how they appear.

Managing notifications helps you stay informed without getting overwhelmed by too many alerts. It's like having a helpful friend who keeps you updated without bothering you too much.

iCloud: Your Data's Home in the Clouds

iCloud is like a virtual storage space that keeps your stuff—photos, files, and more—available on all your Apple devices.

Here's how to get started:

1. Set Up iCloud on your iPhone

    - Open Settings ⚙️, tap on your name at the top, then select iCloud.

    - Turn on the features you want to use, like iCloud Photos or iCloud Drive.

2. Backup your iPhone

    - In Settings ⚙️, go to [Your Name] > iCloud > iCloud Backup.

    - Switch on iCloud Backup to automatically save your iPhone's data.

    - Your iPhone will back up to iCloud when it's connected to Wi-Fi, charging, and locked. You can also do a manual backup anytime.

3. Managing iCloud storage

    • If your iCloud space is full, you can:

        ▪ Delete things you don't need from iCloud.

        ▪ Get more iCloud storage by buying extra space.

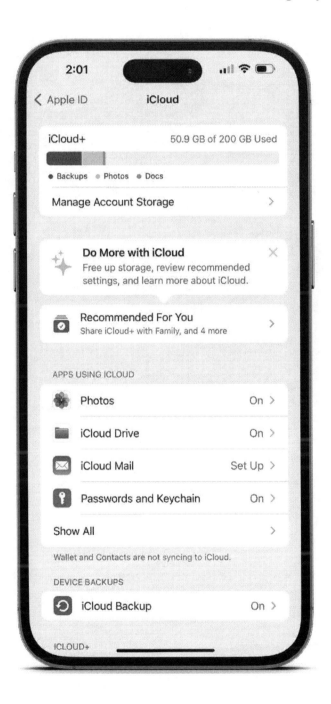

• Try other services like Google Drive, Dropbox, or OneDrive. They all offer different features, prices, and storage sizes, so you can pick what suits you best

• If your iCloud storage is full or you prefer an alternative service, you have options such as deleting unnecessary data from iCloud, buying more iCloud storage, or using other cloud services like Google Drive, Dropbox, or OneDrive. Each of these services has its features, pricing, and storage capacities, so you can choose the one that best suits your needs.

The Control Center: Easy Access to Key Functions

The Control Center is like a toolbox filled with handy tools right at your fingertips. It helps you quickly adjust settings and use features without digging through your phone's settings menu.

How to Access the Control Center

1. Swipe down from the top right corner of your screen.

2. You'll see a panel with icons and sliders. Tap on icons or drag sliders to adjust settings like brightness or volume. Some icons give you more options if you press and hold them.

3. To close the Control Center, swipe up from the bottom of the screen or tap anywhere outside the panel.

Customizing Your Control Center

1. Go to the Settings  App > Locate the Control Center and tap to access the below screen.

2. Tap the plus button next to a control to add it or tap the minus button to remove it.

3. You can also rearrange controls by touching and holding the three lines next to the control, then moving it where you want.

What You Can Add to Your Control Center

You have a bunch of controls to choose from:

- Accessibility Shortcuts

- Apple TV Remote

- Dark Mode

- Do Not Disturb While Driving

- Low Power Mode

- Magnifier

- Screen Recording, and more

Customizing the Control Center helps make it your go-to place for all the tools and settings you use the most, making your iPhone even more convenient to use.

QR Code Scanner

The iPhone simplifies QR code scanning with its built-in feature, accessible through the Camera app or the Control Center. Here's how you can set up the Code Scanner shortcut in the Control Center.

1. Launch the Settings app and tap Control Center.

2. Select Customize Controls.

3. Scroll down to More Controls and locate Code Scanner.

4. Tap the white plus sign next to Code Scanner to add it.

5. You'll now find Code Scanner under Included Controls in the Control Center.

Once you've added the Code Scanner, here's how you can use it to swiftly scan QR codes:

1. Swipe down from the top-right corner of your iPhone screen (or swipe up from the bottom for iPhones with a Home button) to access the Control Center.

2. Tap the QR code icon within the Control Center to activate the dedicated QR code scanning mode in your Camera app.

3. Hover your iPhone over the QR code, follow the on-screen prompts, and voilà! Your iPhone will automatically launch the associated app or website linked to the QR code.

Personalizing Your iPhone's Settings: Making It Your Own

The Settings app on your iPhone is like a control room where you can tweak and adjust your device to suit your preferences. It's all about making your iPhone comfortable and just the way you want it.

Note: **These personalization settings will be covered in greater detail in Chapter 8**

1. **For Improved Visibility and Comfort**

   A. Use Display Zoom: Make icons and text bigger on your Home Screen and in apps.

   B. Go to Settings ⚙ > Display & Brightness > View > Tap "Zoomed" > Tap "Set."

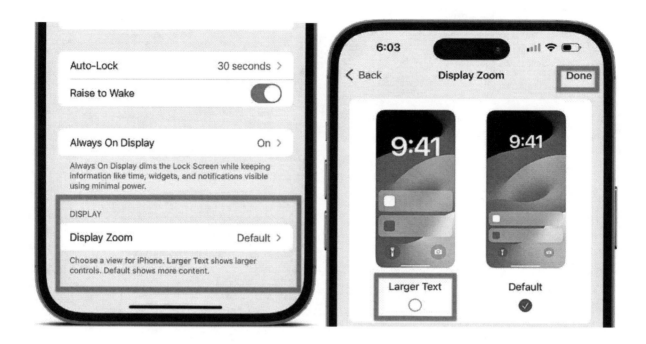

2. **Increase Text Size**: Make text larger in apps like Mail and Messages.

- Go to Settings ⚙ > Accessibility > Display & Text Size > Drag the Text Size slider.

- Turn on Larger Accessibility Sizes for even bigger text

3. Enhancing Accessibility

Speak Selection: Have your iPhone read text aloud.

- Go to Settings 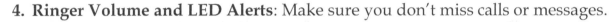 > Accessibility > Spoken Content > Turn on Speak Selection.

- Adjust settings like speaking rate and voice.

4. Ringer Volume and LED Alerts: Make sure you don't miss calls or messages.

- Go to Settings > Sounds & Haptics > Adjust Ringer and Alerts.

- Turn on LED Flash for Alerts in Settings > Accessibility > Audio/Visual.

5. Emergency Features for Safety

A. **Medical ID:** Store important medical info accessible from the Lock Screen.

B. Open the Health app > Tap your profile picture > Tap Medical ID > Enter your information and turn on Show When Locked.

C. **Emergency SOS:** Quickly call emergency services and notify your emergency contacts.

D. Go to Settings 🔘 > Emergency SOS > Turn on Auto Call and set up your emergency contacts.

6. Zoom for Better Vision

Adjust Zoom Settings: Magnify your screen for easier viewing.

- Go to Settings  > Accessibility > Zoom > Turn on Zoom.

- Customize settings like zoom level and navigation gestures.

By adjusting these settings, your iPhone becomes more comfortable, safer, and easier to use, no matter your needs or preferences.

Securing Your Phone: Protecting Your Data

Your Apple ID is your gateway to Apple's ecosystem, offering access to services like the App Store, iCloud, iMessage, FaceTime, and more. You can manage your Apple ID and iCloud storage directly from your iPhone.

Setting a Passcode

- Go to Settings  > Face ID & Passcode (or Touch ID & Passcode for older devices).

- Enter your current passcode or tap Turn Passcode On if it's not enabled.

- To change the passcode, tap Change Passcode and follow the steps. You can also choose a custom numeric or alphanumeric code by tapping Passcode Options.

Managing Privacy and Security

Go to Settings 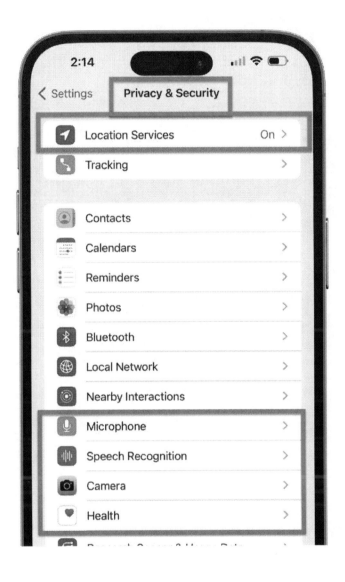 > Privacy.

- Tap on a category like Location Services, Camera, Microphone, or Contacts.

- See the apps that want access to that category and decide which apps you want to grant or revoke permission to.

- Review an app's access permissions by tapping on the app to see all the categories it has requested access to, then adjust permissions as needed.

- These settings are your guardrails to keep your data safe and control what apps can access. Adjust them according to your comfort and preference for added security and peace of mind.

Dark Mode: Making Your iPhone Easier on the Eyes

Dark Mode changes how your iPhone looks, making it darker and easier on your eyes, especially in low light. It's available on iOS 13 and later versions and can even save battery levels on certain iPhone models.

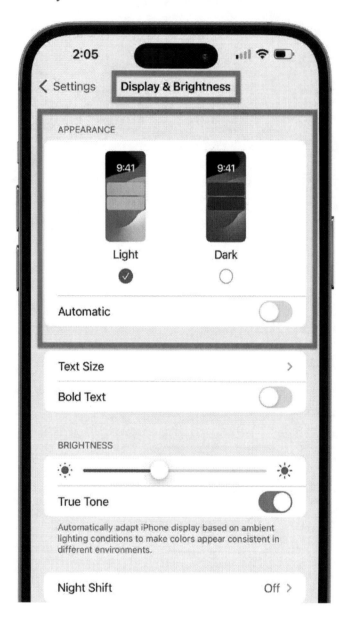

Here's how to turn on Dark Mode:

- Open Settings ⚙ on your iPhone.

- Tap Display & Brightness.

- Choose Dark to turn on Dark Mode.

You can also set Dark Mode to turn on and off automatically at specific times or switch between Light and Dark modes quickly using Control Center. Using Dark Mode can make your iPhone more comfortable to use, especially when it's dark around you. Give it a try to see if it suits your preferences!

Finding Your Lost iPhone

Losing your iPhone is tough, but the Find My app can help you locate it and secure your information remotely.

Follow these steps:

Enable Find My iPhone

- Go to Settings  > [Your Name] > Find My > Find My iPhone and switch it on.

- Make sure your lost iPhone is connected to the internet.

Using the Find My App (on Another Apple Device)

- Open the Find My app on another Apple device, like an iPad or Mac.

- Sign in with your Apple ID and password.

- Tap Devices to see a list, then tap your lost iPhone to view its location on a map.

Actions You Can Take

- Play Sound: Make your iPhone play a loud sound, even if it's on silent mode, to help find it nearby.

- Get Directions: Use the Maps app to get directions to your iPhone's location.

- Mark As Lost: Lock your iPhone with a passcode and show a message with your phone number on the Lock Screen. You can also enable Lost Mode, which disables Apple Pay.

Using the Find My Website (on a Browser)

- Visit iCloud.com/find on a web browser.

- Sign in with your Apple ID and password.

- Follow the steps above, such as playing a sound or marking your device as lost.

- These steps can improve your chances of finding your lost iPhone or keeping your data safe if someone else finds it.

The Importance of Updating Your iPhone

Regular updates are essential for your iPhone's performance, security, and features.

Performance and stability: Updates improve your device's performance, fix bugs, and make it more stable, ensuring a smoother experience.

Security: They include security patches that protect your data from potential threats and vulnerabilities.

New features: Updates often bring new features like Dark Mode, Widgets, and more, enhancing your device's capabilities.

How do you update your phone?

1. Go to Settings ⚙ > General > Software Update.

2. You can enable Automatic Updates to install updates when your device is on Wi-Fi and charging.

Safety tip: Back up your data using iCloud or other cloud services before updating in case of any issues.

Regular updates improve performance, safeguard your data, and introduce new features. Easily manage updates and settings in the Settings app.

For more information on how to update your phone:

- Learn about iOS 17 accessibility Updates in Chapter 8

- Utilize the built-in privacy and security protections of the iPhone

- Additional details and tips on keeping your iPhone in top shape are covered in chapter 10, the final chapter in this book.

FAQs: Home Screen

Q: What's the Home Screen?

A: It's the main iPhone screen displaying apps, widgets, and folders. Swipe left or right for multiple pages.

Q: How can I rearrange apps?

A: Touch and hold an app, drag to rearrange, or tap Remove to delete. Move to edges to switch pages or Dock (see Chapter 5 for more details).

Q: Creating folders?

A: Drag one app over another to create a folder. Add more apps, and rename by tapping the folder's name. (see Chapter 5 for more details).

Q: Using widgets?

A: Touch and hold an empty area, tap Add, choose a widget, select size, and position on the Home Screen.

Q: Accessing App Library?

A: Swipe left until the last page or use the search. Tap categories or apps to open or launch.

For additional help:

- Explore a Getting Started Tour of your iPhone using the **Tips app**

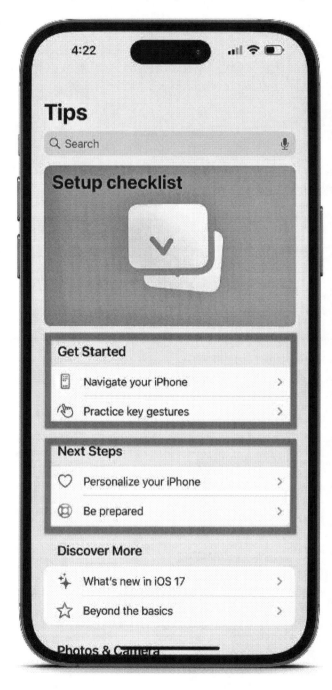 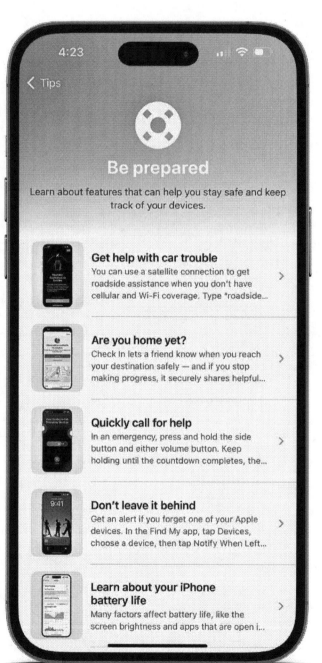

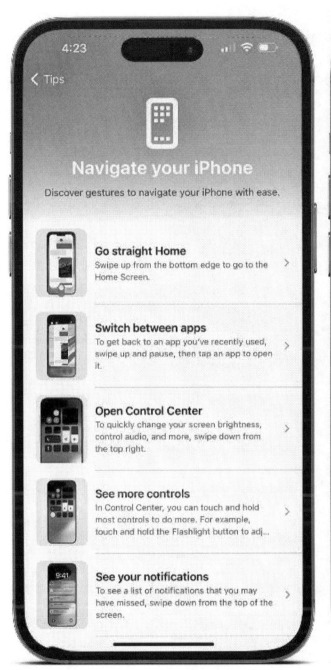

Navigate your iPhone

Discover gestures to navigate your iPhone with ease.

Go straight Home
Swipe up from the bottom edge to go to the Home Screen. >

Switch between apps
To get back to an app you've recently used, swipe up and pause, then tap an app to open it. >

Open Control Center
To quickly change your screen brightness, control audio, and more, swipe down from the top right. >

See more controls
In Control Center, you can touch and hold most controls to do more. For example, touch and hold the Flashlight button to adj... >

See your notifications
To see a list of notifications that you may have missed, swipe down from the top of the screen. >

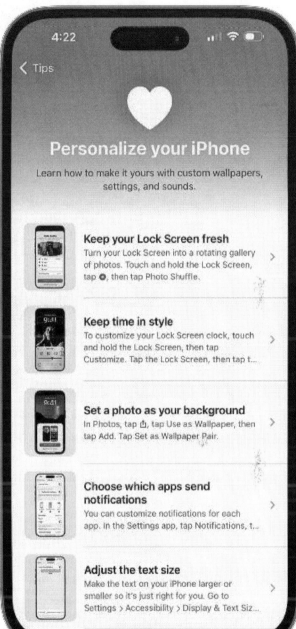

Personalize your iPhone

Learn how to make it yours with custom wallpapers, settings, and sounds.

Keep your Lock Screen fresh
Turn your Lock Screen into a rotating gallery of photos. Touch and hold the Lock Screen, tap ⊙, then tap Photo Shuffle. >

Keep time in style
To customize your Lock Screen clock, touch and hold the Lock Screen, then tap Customize. Tap the Lock Screen, then tap t... >

Set a photo as your background
In Photos, tap ⬆, tap Use as Wallpaper, then tap Add. Tap Set as Wallpaper Pair. >

Choose which apps send notifications
You can customize notifications for each app. In the Settings app, tap Notifications, t... >

Adjust the text size
Make the text on your iPhone larger or smaller so it's just right for you. Go to Settings > Accessibility > Display & Text Siz... >

- Check out iPhone basics for seniors: 7 valuable tips and settings | Seasons Retirement Communities

Regular updates keep your iPhone in top shape while knowing your Home Screen features enhances your experience and organization.

CHAPTER 3

Dialing Into Connectivity: Mastering Calls and Texts on Your iPhone

Smartphones are miracles, and they've turned us into gods. But in one simple respect, they're primitive: you can't slam down the receiver.
—Richard Powers

Ever wished you could dramatically hang up on someone with a smartphone? Unfortunately, that feature hasn't made it into these miraculous devices, as Richard Powers said. Your iPhone might not have the dramatic hang-up feature, but it's a powerful tool for fostering connections. Let's dive into the world of communication with your iPhone.

- Making and receiving calls: Master the art of making and answering calls effortlessly. Explore features like call waiting, forwarding, and using your contacts to simplify the calling experience.

- Texting with ease: Learn the ins and outs of texting on your iPhone. From composing messages to using emojis and sending multimedia, discover how to craft engaging and expressive texts.

- Managing contacts: Uncover the intricacies of managing your contacts. Learn how to add, edit, and organize contacts, ensuring that your address book remains updated and easily accessible.

- Mastering voicemail: Navigate the world of voicemail, from setting it up to retrieving and managing messages. Personalize your voicemail greeting and effortlessly handle incoming messages.

By the end of this chapter, you'll wield essential skills in calling, texting, contact management, and voicemail handling on your iPhone. These abilities will empower you to connect seamlessly with your loved ones, leveraging your iPhone's capabilities to enrich every interaction. Communication becomes a breeze with your iPhone as your trusty companion!

The Art of Dialing: Making and Receiving Calls

Using the Phone app on your iPhone is easier than you think. It has big buttons and a simple layout, making calling a breeze.

Finding the Phone app is simple: Just look for an icon that resembles an old-fashioned telephone receiver on a green background. It's usually at the bottom of your home screen for quick access.

Once you're in the app, making a call is straightforward. You can either dial a number manually or select a contact from your list with just a tap.

Here's how to make calls using different methods.

1. Dial a number manually

Tap the "Keypad" tab in the Phone app. Use the keypad to enter the number. If you make a mistake, tap the delete button. For pauses, hard stops, or international calls, touch and hold the corresponding key. Finally, tap the green call button to start the call.

2. Call a contact

Tap the "Contacts" tab, find the contact, and tap their name. Then tap the phone number you want to call.

3. Call a favorite

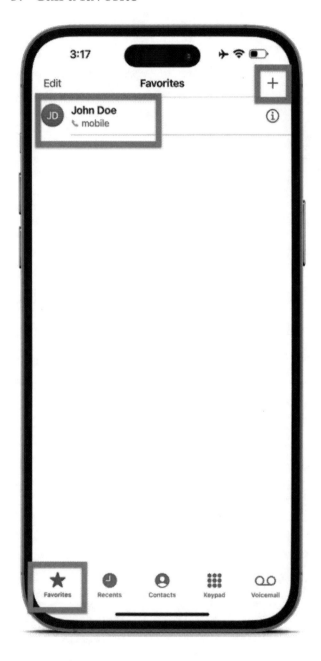

Tap the "Favorites" tab, then the person's name to call them. You can edit your favorites by tapping "Edit" at the top right.

4. Call a recent caller

   Tap the "Recents" tab, find the person, and tap their name or number. You can also see call details and **block the caller**.

5. Call with Siri

Use Siri by holding the side or home button (or saying "Hey Siri").

Say something like "Call John Smith" or "Dial 555-1234." Siri will confirm and start the call.

With these methods, making calls becomes simple and quick, helping you stay connected effortlessly.

Answering Calls on Your iPhone

Receiving calls is simple on your iPhone. When someone calls, their name or number pops up on the screen, and you'll see two buttons: green for answering and red for declining.

Here's what to do:

1. To decline a call

   If you're busy or not in the mood to chat, tap the red button. The call will go to voicemail, and you can set up your own message later on.

2. To answer a call

   Tap the green button. Hold the phone to your ear as you would with a regular phone. You'll hear the caller through the earpiece, and they'll hear you through the microphone at the bottom of the phone.

Using Speakerphone

For hands-free calls, tap the green button, then tap the speaker icon at the bottom left. This allows you to talk and listen without holding the phone to your ear. You'll hear the caller through the bottom speaker, and they'll hear you through the top microphone. You can also use headphones or a Bluetooth device for hands-free talking.

Turn on the speakerphone before making a call.

1. Open the Phone app.

2. Tap the speaker icon at the top right. It'll turn blue to indicate it's on.

3. Then, dial the number or select a contact as usual to start the call. You'll hear the ringing and the caller's voice through the speaker.

To turn on the speakerphone during a call:

1. While on a call, tap the speaker icon at the bottom left.

2. The icon turns blue, indicating the speakerphone is active. You can switch back to the earpiece or headphones by tapping the icon again.

Use the mute button as required

With these steps, answering calls and using the speakerphone feature becomes a breeze on your iPhone.

Managing Your Contacts on Your iPhone

Your contacts on your iPhone include everyone you communicate with, like family, friends, or colleagues. Let's see how you can manage the contacts on your phone.

The Contacts app on your iPhone is a robust tool that streamlines contact management. It allows you to save phone numbers, emails, and comprehensive details about your contacts in an organized manner. From the app, you can Initiate calls, messages, FaceTime calls, or share contact information directly from the Contacts app for a more efficient communication process. Efficiently organize and locate contacts, ensuring quick access whenever required.

Adding a Contact

1. Open the Contacts or Phone app and tap the plus (+) button at the top right.

2. Enter the contact's details like name, phone number, email, and more. You can also add a photo.

3. Tap Done to save the contact.

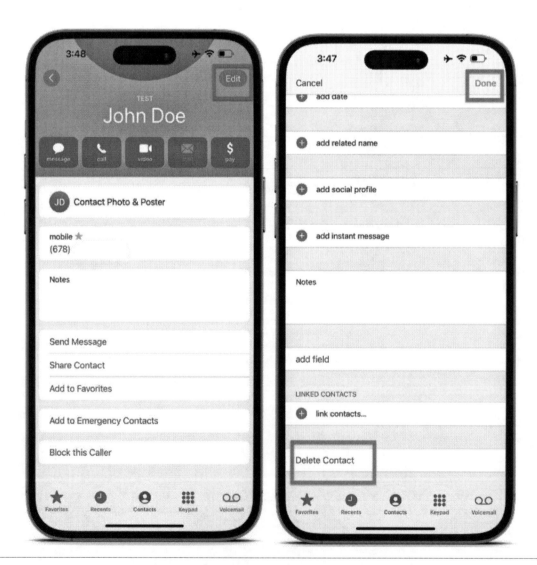

Editing a Contact

1. Open the Contacts or Phone app and select the contact you want to edit.

2. Tap Edit at the top right.

3. Make the changes you need, like adding or deleting info, changing the name or photo, or setting a ringtone.

4. Tap Done to save the changes.

Deleting a Contact

1. Open the Contacts or Phone app and select the contact you want to delete.

2. Tap Edit at the top right.

3. Scroll down and tap Delete Contact, then confirm to delete it permanently from your iPhone and synced devices.

Communicating From the App

Tap a contact's name within the app to access various communication options, including calls, messages, FaceTime calls, or sharing their contact information.

Organizing Contacts Into Groups

Create groups to categorize contacts for easier management. Tap "Edit," then "Add Group," assign a name, choose the storage location, and add or remove contacts as needed.

Efficient Contact Search

Utilize the search bar to find specific contacts by their name, phone number, or email. Tap a contact's name to view detailed information or initiate direct calls or messages.

The Contacts app simplifies contact management, facilitating seamless connections with family and friends. Whether adding new contacts, updating information, or quickly finding specific contacts, this app ensures a smooth and hassle-free experience.

Organizing Contacts Into Lists

1. Open the Contacts or Phone app and tap the Lists button at the top left.

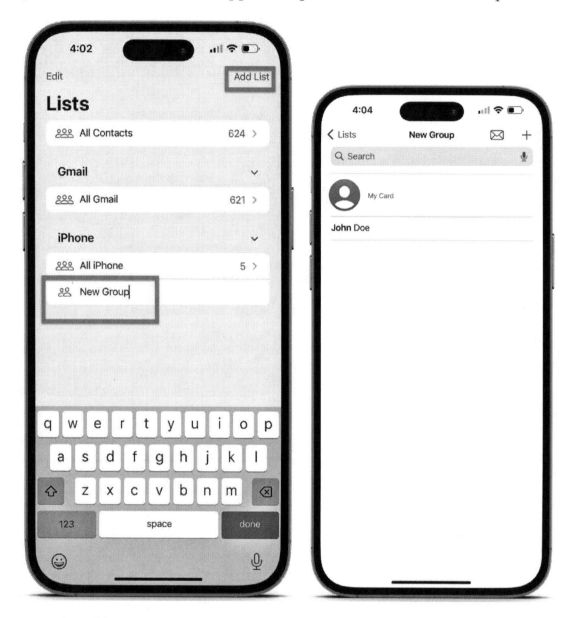

2. Create lists like Family, Friends, or Work by tapping the plus (+) button. Name the list and choose where to save it.

3. To add contacts to a list, tap the list's name, then Add Contacts and choose the contacts to add.

4. To remove contacts from a list, tap the list, tap Edit, and then tap the minus (-) button next to the contacts you want to remove.

With these steps, managing your contacts becomes simple on your iPhone.

Checking Voicemail

Voicemail lets callers leave recorded messages when you can't answer. Here's how to manage your voicemail:

Listening to Voicemail

1. Open the Phone app and tap the Voicemail tab at the bottom right.

2. You'll see a list of messages with caller info, date, time, and duration.

3. Tap a message to listen. Use the play button, speaker icon for speakerphone, trash icon to delete, or share icon to save or send the message.

Setting Up Greeting

1. In the Phone app, tap Voicemail and then Greeting at the top left. There are two options you can choose from:

   Default: Uses a standard greeting like "You've reached [your number]. Please leave a message."

   Custom: Record your own greeting. Tap Record, say your message, then tap Stop. Listen, and if satisfied, tap Save.

By following these steps, you can manage your voicemail easily on your iPhone.

The Art of Texting: Sending and Receiving Messages

Texting is another way to communicate with your contacts on your iPhone. You can use the Messages app to send and receive text messages, photos, videos, emojis, stickers, and more. You can also use iMessage, a free service that lets you send messages over Wi-Fi or cellular data to other iPhone, iPad, iPod touch, or Mac users, or FaceTime, a free service that lets you make video or audio calls over Wi-Fi or cellular data to other Apple devices. In this section, you'll learn how to send and receive messages, use iMessage and FaceTime, and manage your conversations on your iPhone.

There are several ways to send and receive messages on your iPhone, depending on how you want to find the person you want to message. Here are some of the most common methods.

Texting on your iPhone is simple and versatile with the Messages app.

Sending a Message

- Open Messages and tap the compose button (top right).

- Enter a contact's name, and number, or tap the plus button to select from your contacts.

- Type your message or use the microphone to dictate.

- Use icons for the camera, photo, emojis, stickers, GIFs, etc.

- Tap send when ready.

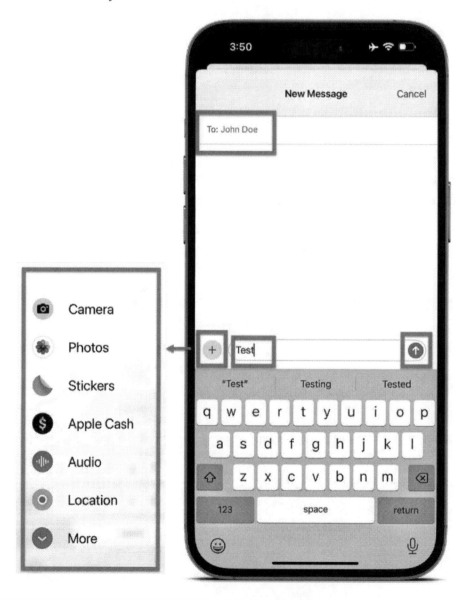

Messaging Recent Contacts

1. Open Messages and tap a conversation.

2. Type a message or reply by holding a message and tapping Reply.

3. Tap the info button for more options like calling or muting the conversation.

Messaging via Siri

Activate Siri and say commands like "Send a message to John Smith" or "Read my messages" to send or receive messages hands-free.

Activate Siri and say commands like "Send a message to John Smith" or "Read my messages" to send or receive messages hands-free.

Using these methods, you can effortlessly send and manage messages on your iPhone.

Using iMessage and FaceTime for Easy Communication

iMessage and FaceTime are handy tools for chatting and calling other Apple users over Wi-Fi or data. Here's how to use them:

iMessage

1. Turn on iMessage in Settings 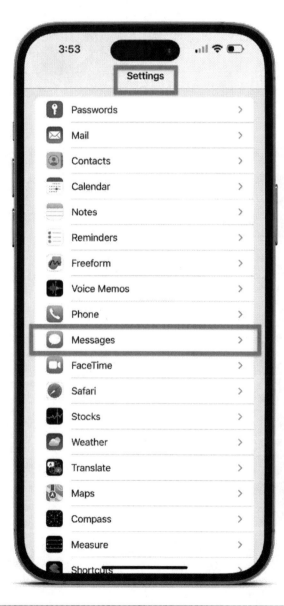 > Messages and sign in with your Apple ID.

2. Select which number or email you want to use for iMessage.

3. Enable Read Receipts to let others know when you've read their messages.

4. Ensure "Send as SMS" is on for sending texts when iMessage isn't available.

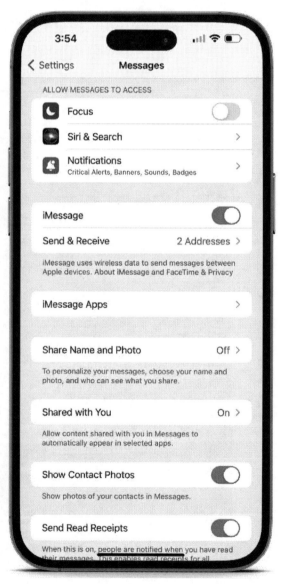

Sending iMessages

1. Just like regular texts, ensure the contact has an Apple device and is signed in with their Apple ID.

2. The blue Send button and text field indicate you're sending an iMessage.

3. Share more than just text: photos, videos, emojis, stickers, GIFs, and use effects for fun chats.

FaceTime

1. Activate FaceTime in Settings ⚙ > FaceTime and sign in with your Apple ID.

2. Choose the number or email for FaceTime calls.

3. Enable FaceTime Live Photos to capture moments during calls.

4. Utilize Calls from iPhone for FaceTime on other devices.

Making FaceTime Calls

1. Open FaceTime, enter a contact's details or select from your list.

2. Start a group FaceTime with up to 32 people by adding multiple contacts.

3. Initiate the call using the video or audio button.

4. Utilize features during the call: switch cameras, mute, add effects, or capture live photos.

With these steps, you can easily connect with friends and family using iMessage and FaceTime.

Managing Conversations on Your iPhone Made Easy

Your iPhone makes managing conversations a breeze.

Delete a conversation: Swipe left on the conversation in Messages, tap the trash icon, then tap Delete to remove it from all synced devices.

Archive a conversation: Swipe left, and tap the folder with a down arrow. Access archived messages through the Lists button and See All. Unarchive by swiping left and tapping the up arrow folder icon.

Pin a conversation: Swipe right, and tap the yellow pushpin icon. Unpin by swiping right and tapping the yellow pushpin with a slash.

Mute a conversation: Swipe left, and tap the bell with a slash icon. Unmute by swiping left and tapping the bell icon.

Mark as read or unread: Swipe right, tap the blue dot, or open the envelope icon to change the status.

Report a conversation: Tap the conversation, then tap the info button. Scroll down and tap Report Junk or Report Spam. You can also block the contact.

Exploring User-Friendly Phone Apps via the App Store

If you're seeking easier-to-use phone apps or want additional features for contact management, the App Store offers a vast array of options.

1. Accessing the App Store – Open the App Store from your home screen, identified by a blue "A" icon.

2. Searching for Apps:

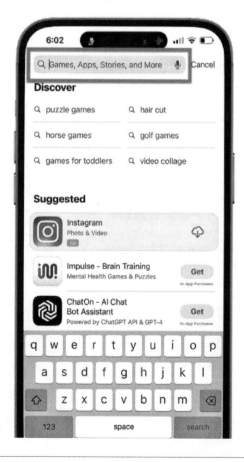

A. Tap "Search" at the bottom right to begin your search.

B. Use keywords like "phone app" or "contacts app" in the search bar.

C. Filter results by category, price, ratings, and age rating using the filter button.

3. App Information

   A. Tap an app from the results to access its details, including features, ratings, reviews, and screenshots.

   B. Explore apps by the same developer or contact them for support.

4. Downloading and Installing

We'll cover the download and install process in much more detail in Chapter 5.

Here are some recommended user-friendly phone apps from the App Store.

1. Phone Contacts Book - Senior and Elderly Citizens

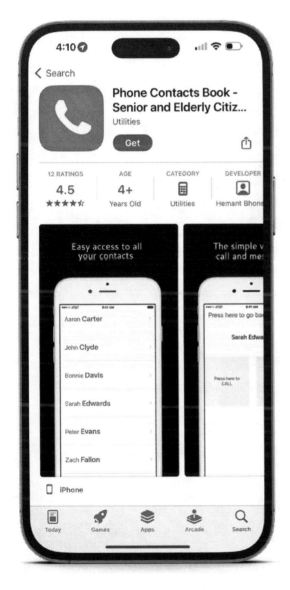

1. Tailored for seniors with easy-to-read fonts, clear icons, and voice feedback.

2. Simple contact management with an emergency feature for reaching emergency contacts

2. Easy Contacts

- Sleek and minimalist design with a powerful search function.

- Features include contact management, smart dialing, and contact backup.

3. Eyecon

- Vibrant app with social media insights and photos for contacts.

- Supports standard contact management tasks, caller ID, and customization.

These apps cater to various preferences, offering simplicity, enhanced accessibility, and engaging visual features for a more personalized calling and contact management experience.

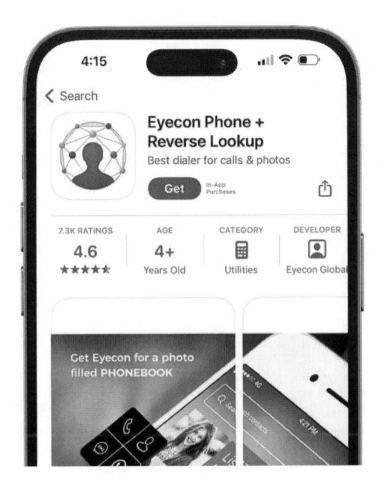

FAQ About Advanced Call Features on iPhone

Q: How do I make a conference call on my iPhone?

A: To initiate a conference call on your iPhone:

1. Start by calling the first participant.

2. Once connected, tap "add call" and dial the second participant's number.

3. Upon their answer, merge the calls by tapping "merge calls."

4. You can repeat these steps to include up to five participants in the conference.

Q: How do I use call waiting on my iPhone?

A: Utilize call waiting to manage multiple calls:

- When a new call arrives while you're on a call, tap "hold and answer" to switch to the new call and put the initial call on hold.

- Use the "swap" button to switch between the two calls.

- Decline the new call by tapping "end and decline" to continue with the ongoing call.

- Alternatively, send the new call to voicemail by tapping "send to voicemail" to retain the current call.

Q: How do I use call forwarding on my iPhone?

A: Redirect incoming calls to another number by enabling call forwarding:

1. Navigate to Settings ⊚ > Phone > Call Forwarding and switch it on.

2. Enter the forwarding number or choose a contact from your list.

3. Select the forwarding condition from options like "Always Forward," "Forward When Busy," "Forward When Unreachable," or "Forward When Unanswered."

Q: How do I use caller ID on my iPhone?

A: Caller ID helps manage incoming calls:

- Identify unknown callers by tapping calls with a question mark in the Phone app's Recents tab.

- Block unwanted callers by accessing a contact's information in the Recents tab and selecting "Block this Caller."

- Hide your own number by disabling "Show My Caller ID" in Settings ⊚ > Phone.

These advanced call features on the iPhone empower efficient call management, customization, and connection facilitation. Understanding these functionalities enhances your iPhone experience, allowing you to tailor calls to your preferences. As you delve further into your device's capabilities, the next chapter will uncover touch gestures and voice commands, empowering you to maximize your iPhone's potential. Get ready to explore and harness your iPhone's full range of capabilities!

CHAPTER 4

Mastering Your iPhone's Language: Touch Gestures and Voice Commands

The most important thing in life is not knowing everything, it's having the phone number of somebody who does!
—Unknown

L et's dive into the language of touch gestures and voice commands, unlocking the secrets to navigate your iPhone with ease and precision, from the fundamental ABCs of tapping, swiping, and pinching to harnessing the power of Siri for hands-free interactions.

- Tapping: Understand the basics of tapping—its uses, applications, and how it's the equivalent of a mouse click in the digital world.

- Swiping: Master the swiping technique to navigate through apps, web pages, and menus with ease.

- Pinching: Explore the two-finger pinch gesture, unlocking the power to zoom in and out effortlessly.

- Navigating with Siri: Learn the magic words—"Hey Siri"—to initiate voice commands. Explore the multitude of tasks Siri can assist with, from making calls and sending messages to setting reminders and controlling smart home devices.

- Effortless iPhone mastery: Ease of Navigation: Discover how combining touch gestures and voice commands streamlines your iPhone experience, making navigation and control intuitive and efficient.

- Precision and seamlessness: Unveil the seamless harmony between touch and voice control, empowering you to wield your iPhone with precision and expertise.

This chapter is your ticket to mastering touch gestures and voice commands, turning your iPhone interaction into an art form. Soon, you'll navigate your device effortlessly and command it with the finesse of a tech pro! Let's embark on this journey to unveil the art of touch and voice control, making your iPhone experience not just intuitive but truly seamless.

The ABCs of Touch Gestures: Tap, Swipe, and Pinch

Mastering touch gestures on your iPhone is like learning the alphabet of its language. Here's a closer look at these fundamental gestures and how they make your iPhone experience intuitive and enjoyable.

Tap: The Essential Interaction	Similar to a computer mouse click, tapping involves lightly pressing your fingertip on the screen.
	Tap is used for various tasks such as opening apps, selecting options, typing, and confirming actions. For example, a single tap on app icons opens them for use, or tapping links in emails or webpages directs you to the linked content.
	iPhone settings offer adjustments for tap sensitivity, enabling customization to accommodate different touch preferences.
Swipe: Effortless Navigation	Swiping involves moving your finger in a specific direction across the screen's surface.
	Swiping up/down enables smooth scrolling through content like web pages or lengthy lists.
	Horizontal swipes facilitate movement between different screens or pages within apps.
	Swipe to scroll through emails or social media feeds and use swipes to switch between screens in apps like Photos or Messages.

Pinch: Zooming Into Detail	Performed by placing two fingers on the screen simultaneously.
	Zoom In/Out: Spread fingers apart to zoom in; bring them closer to zoom out.
	Detail magnification: This enables a closer look at smaller elements within images, texts, or maps.
	Or you can use the pinch gesture to zoom in on photos for detailed examination. Zoom in on text for easier reading, especially for smaller fonts.

These touch gestures form the backbone of interacting with your iPhone. Mastering their functionalities allows for seamless navigation and exploration throughout various applications and activities on your device.

Understanding and practicing these gestures is like learning the foundation of a new language. Embrace the simplicity and functionality they offer by experimenting with different apps and scenarios. It'll unlock a more seamless and enjoyable iPhone experience!

Open any app or webpage and practice tapping icons, swiping through content, and pinching to zoom in and out. Experiment with different directions and motions until these gestures feel natural and effortless. Continuously practice these gestures within various apps and contexts to enhance familiarity and ease of use.

Experiment with variations in speed and pressure to understand how these gestures respond to your touch.

Mastering these fundamental touch gestures forms the bedrock of effortless navigation on your iPhone. Regular practice and experimentation across different apps and scenarios will cultivate proficiency and comfort with these gestures.

To practice, open any app or webpage and try tapping icons, swiping through content, and pinching to zoom in and out. Experiment with different directions and motions until you feel comfortable using these gestures effortlessly.

Adjusting Touch Sensitivity

Adjusting touch sensitivity can greatly impact your iPhone usage, especially for those seeking a specific touch response. Here's how you can fine-tune touch settings and explore alternatives for a more personalized experience.

Accessibility Settings

1. Go to Settings ⚙ on your iPhone.

2. Tap on Accessibility.

3. Select the Touch option.

4. Explore "Touch Accommodations" to find features that allow modifications in touch sensitivity, duration, or hold duration. This customization caters to individual preferences for touch interaction.

AssistiveTouch

1. Access Settings ⚙ on your iPhone.

2. Tap on Accessibility.

3. Select the Touch option.

4. Enable AssistiveTouch, which creates a virtual touch interface on your screen.

5. Customize the sensitivity settings within AssistiveTouch to suit your preferred touch response.

6. Additionally, you can create custom gestures that align with your comfort level and interaction style.

Third-Party Apps

1. Visit the App Store on your iPhone.

2. Search for apps specifically designed to modify touch sensitivity or provide alternative touch interfaces.

3. Explore and try out different apps available, as some offer customizable touch settings or gesture recognition tailored to specific needs. Look for apps that cater to senior-friendly options, if applicable.

It's important to note that there are different screen protectors or cases available in the market and some of them might impact the feel of the screen, potentially affecting touch sensitivity. Experiment with different screen protectors or cases to find one that offers a more suitable touch experience, aligning with your sensitivity preferences.

Exploring these options allows you to fine-tune touch sensitivity according to your comfort and requirements. Experimenting with settings, features, apps, or accessories ensures a more tailored and enjoyable touch interaction experience on your iPhone.

Utilizing Siri for Voice Commands

Siri, Apple's renowned voice assistant, revolutionizes iPhone interaction by enabling hands-free device management through voice commands, streamlining tasks, and enhancing multitasking capabilities.

It acts as your voice-activated assistant, facilitating the hands-free operation of your iPhone. Siri enables a range of functionalities, including task execution, information retrieval, and device control, all through voice commands.

You can summon Siri in two primary ways:

- "Hey Siri" voice activation: Start Siri by simply saying "Hey Siri" aloud. This hands-free method allows instant access without touching the device.

- Physical activation: Alternatively, press and hold the side (depending on your iPhone model) to activate Siri.

Siri's activation methods offer flexibility, catering to varied user preferences and accessibility needs. Once activated, Siri seamlessly integrates into your iPhone usage, offering a hands-free approach to managing tasks and accessing information swiftly.

Activating Siri

1. Ensure Siri is enabled

   A. Go to your iPhone's Settings ⚙.

   B. Tap on "Siri & Search."

   C. Toggle on "Listen for 'Hey Siri.'"

2. Summon Siri

   A. Say "Hey Siri" aloud in a clear voice.

   B. Wait for Siri's activation chime or visual response (depending on your device settings).

Activating Siri via Button

1. Locate the side button

   A. For iPhone X and later models, it's the side button on the right.

2. Press and Hold the button

   A. Firmly press and hold the side or home button for a couple of seconds.

3. Wait for Siri's activation

   A. Siri will appear on the screen or respond audibly, indicating activation.

Using either method, you can seamlessly activate Siri and start issuing voice commands or inquiries, allowing hands-free interaction with your iPhone. Adjust Siri settings as needed to ensure optimal functionality.

Tasks With Siri

Siri is equipped to handle a variety of tasks on your iPhone, offering a seamless and hands-free experience across multiple functionalities.

Making Calls

Siri simplifies the process of initiating phone calls with voice commands. For instance, using the "Hey Siri" command, you can say something like "Call Mark" or "Call Mark at home" to prompt Siri to dial the specified contact. This feature is especially beneficial when driving, cooking, or engaging in activities where hands-free operation is essential for safety or convenience.

Sending Messages

Siri enables hands-free composing and sending of text messages or emails. For instance, by saying "Send a message to John," Siri prompts you to dictate the content of the message, allowing you to send texts without typing. This is useful when you're occupied and need to communicate quickly, especially for individuals with limited dexterity or visual impairments.

Setting Reminders

Managing your schedule becomes easier with Siri's assistance in setting reminders. For example, by commanding Siri to "Remind me to buy groceries at 5 p.m.," Siri will schedule a reminder for the specified task at the designated time. This function comes in handy especially if you need reminders for medication schedules, appointments, or daily tasks, enhancing organization and time management.

Weather Updates and Information Retrieval

Siri provides instant access to information, including weather forecasts, news updates, or specific information without navigating apps or websites. Ask Siri questions like "What's the weather like today?" or "What's the news?" to receive quick, spoken responses without having to navigate through various apps.

Navigation Assistance

Siri offers navigational support by providing directions through voice commands. Ask Siri for directions to a specific location or ask about nearby restaurants, gas stations, or points of interest, making it helpful while driving or exploring new areas.

Entertainment and Leisure

Siri assists in various leisure activities, such as playing music or setting reminders for TV shows or events. Ask Siri to play specific songs, artists, or genres, enhancing your entertainment experience hands-free. Schedule reminders for your favorite TV shows or events, ensuring you don't miss out on entertainment you love.

Personal Assistance and Task Management

Siri acts as a personal assistant, managing appointments, creating shopping lists, or providing quick information. Command Siri to add items to your shopping list or set reminders for important tasks, assisting in daily organization and productivity.

Siri's multifaceted capabilities cater to a wide range of needs and preferences, offering convenience, accessibility, and efficiency in everyday tasks. Whether it's managing schedules, communicating hands-free, or accessing information swiftly, Siri aims to enhance the user experience on your iPhone through intuitive voice commands.

These functions represent just a fraction of Siri's capabilities. Siri continues to evolve with new features and integrations, making it a versatile tool for managing various tasks and accessing information on your iPhone. And it is customizable.

Smart Home Control

Siri acts as a hub for managing smart home devices that are compatible with Apple's HomeKit ecosystem.

Using voice commands, you can control various smart home devices:

- Lighting control: Turn on/off lights or adjust brightness levels by commanding Siri.

- Thermostat adjustment: Change temperature settings on smart thermostats.

- Locks and security: Lock or unlock doors, check security cameras, or activate alarm systems if they are HomeKit-enabled.

App-Specific Commands

Siri integrates with certain apps to execute specific actions without manual interaction. Users can employ Siri to perform tasks within supported applications, such as ordering a ride through a ridesharing app or sending money via a payment app, all through voice commands.

Device Control

Siri facilitates managing various system settings and functionalities on your iPhone or other Apple devices. Control various device settings without manually navigating through menus. Adjust screen brightness, enable/disable Bluetooth, activate the "Do Not Disturb" mode, change volume, and more through voice commands.

Knowledge and Information

Siri functions as a versatile information resource, capable of answering various queries and providing instant information. Ask Siri for information on facts, calculations, conversions, definitions, weather updates, sports scores, stock prices, and more.

Integration With Third-Party Apps

Siri collaborates with numerous third-party applications, enabling users to initiate specific actions within these apps via voice commands. Some applications have integrated Siri functionality, allowing users to perform tasks within these apps without manually navigating through them.

Shortcuts and Automation

Users can create personalized shortcuts for Siri to execute multiple tasks with a single voice command. Set up custom commands to perform a series of actions across various apps or system functionalities, enhancing productivity and convenience.

Multilingual Support

Siri can comprehend and respond to commands in multiple languages, providing a broader range of users with access to its capabilities. Users can interact with Siri in different languages, facilitating more inclusive user experiences.

Contextual Awareness

Siri's responses can adapt based on context or ongoing conversations, making interactions more intuitive and conversational. Siri's understanding of context allows for more natural interactions, and understanding of follow-up questions or commands based on prior dialogue.

Accessibility Features

Siri supports various accessibility features, aiding users with disabilities in navigating and using their devices more effectively. Siri collaborates with accessibility features like

VoiceOver and AssistiveTouch, making the device more accessible and user-friendly for individuals with disabilities.

Regular updates to iOS often bring enhancements and new features to Siri, making it crucial to explore and stay updated with Siri's capabilities to fully leverage its functionalities and enhance your iPhone experience.

Customize Siri

Customizing Siri allows you to fine-tune the voice assistant to suit your preferences and enhance your overall experience.

Here's a look at how you can personalize Siri for your own personal needs.

Language and Voice Customization

1. Access the Settings ⚙ app on your iPhone, and Navigate to "Siri and Search."

2. Choosing Siri Voice and Language:

   A. Tap on "Siri Voice" within the "Siri and Search" settings.

   B. From the available options, select your preferred language and voice for Siri. This customization allows you to interact with Siri in a language and voice tone that suits you best.

Allowing Siri When Locked

1. Accessing Siri & Search Settings

   A. Return to the "Siri and Search" section in your Settings app.

2. Enabling Siri When Locked

   A. Locate and enable the setting labeled "Allow Siri When Locked."

   B. Enabling this option permits Siri to function even when your iPhone is locked, facilitating hands-free interaction with Siri without unlocking your device.

Adjusting Voice Feedback

1. Returning to Siri & Search Settings

    A. Once again, navigate back to the "Siri and Search" settings.

2. Accessing Voice Feedback Options

    A. Look for the option named "Voice Feedback" within the Siri and Search settings.

    B. Here, you can choose between spoken responses or text-only responses based on your preference.

    C. This customization allows you to decide whether Siri responds audibly or with text-only feedback.

Personalized Experience Over Time

As you regularly interact with Siri for various tasks and inquiries, the voice assistant learns from your habits, preferences, and usage patterns. Over time, Siri's AI learns and adapts to your behavior, providing tailored assistance. Based on your interactions, Siri starts to offer personalized suggestions, reminders, and assistance that align with your routines and preferences. The more you engage with Siri, the better it becomes at understanding your needs, enhancing its ability to provide relevant and timely information, and making your iPhone usage more intuitive and efficient.

CHAPTER 5

A Walkthrough of the App Store: Your Gateway to New Experiences

Apple's App Store has 1.76 million apps and 460,000 games and free apps make up 94.1% of the Apple App Store.
—David Curry

The App Store serves as an expansive marketplace within your iPhone's ecosystem, granting access to a plethora of applications tailored to diverse interests and needs.

To access the App Store, tap on the blue letter "A" on your phone's home screen.

Tapping this icon launches the App Store, opening the gateway to a vast array of applications. This might be overwhelming at first, but I'll guide you through and by the end, you'll be a master of this digital store.

Think of the App Store as a massive digital mall, housing various shops, each representing an app tailored to different interests and functionalities. It's an extensive repository catering to virtually every aspect of your life. Upon entering, you'll notice tabs at the bottom of the screen: "Today," "Games," "Apps," and more. These tabs act as your navigation menu, guiding you through the store's offerings.

The search tool, denoted by a magnifying glass icon, empowers you to find specific apps swiftly. Simply tap the icon, input the app's name or category, and explore the search results.

The "Today" and "Apps" tabs are treasure troves for discovering new apps. "Today" highlights featured apps, editor's picks, and insightful stories. Meanwhile, the "Apps" section enables exploration across diverse categories.

The App Store cleverly tailors recommendations based on your interests and frequently used apps. These personalized suggestions mimic a helpful shopping assistant, proposing items aligned with your preferences. You'll find these recommendations in the "Today" and "Apps" tabs.

The App Store's user-friendly interface and tailored suggestions make finding, exploring, and discovering new apps an effortless and enjoyable experience.

Free apps are often enticing, offering immediate access without an upfront cost. However, they may come with certain drawbacks that users should be aware of. Here's a more detailed look at the differences between free and paid apps, as well as essential steps for setting up your digital account and downloading apps.

Free vs. Paid Apps

Free Apps: These apps are accessible at no initial cost but might include advertisements or have limited functionality. They might prompt users to make in-app purchases or you will have to subscribe for full access to the app and to remove the ads.

Paid Apps: These display a price instead of the "Get" button. These apps are considered premium, and they often offer additional features, an ad-free experience, or more comprehensive functionalities.

To download and purchase an app from the App Store you will need an Apple ID

Apple ID Setup

An Apple ID is your gateway to Apple's ecosystem, essential for various functionalities on your iPhone, including app downloads from the App Store.

Follow these steps to create or sign in to your Apple ID via Settings:

1. Accessing Apple ID Settings

    - Open your iPhone's Settings app.

    - Tap on [Your Name] at the top of the Settings menu.

2. Accessing iTunes & App Store

    - Scroll down and select iTunes & App Store.

    - If you don't have an Apple ID, tap "Create New Apple ID" and follow the prompts to set up your account with an email address, password, security questions, and billing information.

    - If you have an existing Apple ID, tap "Sign In" and enter your Apple ID credentials to link it to your device.

3. Verification

- You might need to verify your identity through a verification code sent to your trusted device or via email to complete the setup.

Apple Pay Setup

Apple Pay offers a secure and convenient payment method for in-store, online, and in-app purchases.

Here's how to set it up:

1. Accessing Apple Pay Settings

- Open the Settings 🌀 app on your iPhone.

- Tap on Wallet & Apple Pay.

2. Adding Credit/Debit Cards

- Select "Add Card" to add your credit or debit cards to Apple Pay.

- Follow the prompts to capture your card's details using the camera or enter them manually.

3. Verification and Authentication

- Verify your card with your bank through authentication methods like a one-time code or by contacting your bank.

Aside from Apple Pay, you can link various payment methods to your Apple ID for app purchases.

- Credit/Debit cards: Add multiple credit or debit cards for payments.

- PayPal: Link your PayPal account for purchases.

- Gift Cards: Redeem gift cards to your Apple ID for app purchases.

To manage these payment methods:

- Go to Settings ⚙ > [Your Name] > iTunes & App Store > Apple ID > Payment & Shipping.

Here, you can add, remove, or edit payment methods associated with your Apple ID for seamless app purchases from the App Store.

Downloading Apps From the App Store

After your Apple ID is set up along with your payment methods, you are ready to begin downloading apps from the App Store.

Follow these easy steps for app downloads:

1. Selecting Apps

- Locate the App: Open the App Store on your iPhone by tapping the blue "A" icon on your home screen.

- Browse or Search: Explore categories or use the search function to find the app you want.

- Free Apps: For free apps, tap the "Get" button.

- Paid Apps: For paid apps, the price will be displayed instead of "Get." Tap the price button to initiate the download.

2. Confirmation

- Authenticate: After tapping "Get" or the price button, a prompt may appear asking you to authenticate the download.

- Authentication Methods: Authenticate using your Apple ID password, Touch ID, or Face ID based on your device's capabilities.

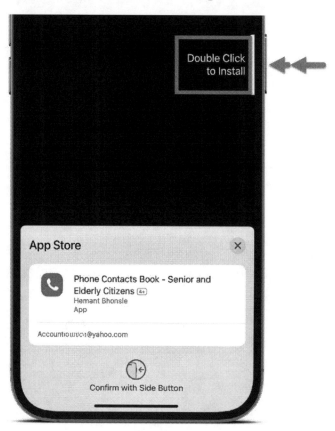

3. Tracking downloads

- Monitor Progress: Once the download starts, you'll see the app icon on your home screen with a loading circle indicating the download progress.

- Check Home Screen: The app's icon will display a loading circle overlay until the download is complete.

- Downloading Time: The time taken for the download depends on the app's size and your internet connection speed.

- Installation: Once downloaded, the app will install automatically and be ready to use.

You're also able to customize your download preferences.

App Store Preferences

1. Automatic Downloads

   - Enable Automatic Downloads: To activate this feature, go to Settings app 🌐 on your iPhone.

   - iTunes & App Store: Tap on [your name] > iTunes & App Store.

   - Enable Automatic Downloads: Toggle on the "Apps" option under Automatic Downloads. When enabled, any apps purchased on other devices linked to your Apple ID will automatically download to your iPhone.

2. Background Downloads

   - Download in Background: While downloading an app, if your iPhone goes idle or locks, the download process may continue in the background automatically without needing you to keep the App Store open.

   - iOS Functionality: Background downloads are an inherent feature of iOS, allowing apps to download and update while the phone is in an idle state.

Managing Downloads

1. Paused Downloads

   - Resuming a Download: If a download is paused or interrupted, you can resume it by tapping the app's icon on the home screen.

   - Tap the App: Locate the app that's currently downloading but paused, then tap on it. This action prompts the app to resume the download process.

2. Viewing the Download Queue

   - Checking Download Progress: To view the download queue when multiple apps are being downloaded or updated simultaneously:

   - App Store Icon: Tap the App Store icon on your iPhone's home screen.

- Updates Section: Navigate to the Updates tab within the App Store to see the list of apps currently downloading or updating.

Troubleshooting Downloads

1. Stuck Downloads

   - Restart iPhone: If an app gets stuck during download or installation, try restarting your iPhone.

   - Force-Quit App Store: Force-quitting the App Store and relaunching it might resolve the issue. Swipe up from the bottom (or swipe up and hold) to reveal the app switcher, then swipe the App Store app card up to force-quit it.

2. Slow Downloads

   - Check Internet Connection: Slow internet speeds can impact download speed. Consider switching to a faster and more stable Wi-Fi network.

   - Wi-Fi Settings: Go to Settings 🔘 > Wi-Fi, then select a different network with better connectivity if available.

These steps should help you manage your app downloads more effectively and troubleshoot any issues that may arise during the process.

The App Store simplifies app downloads, providing a streamlined process to add new functionalities and entertainment options to your iPhone. Tracking download progress ensures you're aware of the status, allowing you to explore and use your newly acquired apps efficiently.

Exploring Useful Apps

The App Store is like a massive mall with sections for everything—kind of like a mall with a '"Productivity Tools" aisle for the busy bees, a "Health and Fitness" corner for the workout warriors, a "Games" arcade for the playful minds, a "Learning Center" for the brainiacs, and an "Entertainment Plaza" for the chillaxers.

To hit up a specific spot in this virtual mall:

1. Head to the "Apps" tab down below.

2. Scroll till you find your zone: "Productivity," "Health & Fitness," "Games," "Education," or "Entertainment."

3. Dive into any zone that tickles your fancy to check out what's hot and happening. They've got the cool stuff — the editors' favorites and the cream of the crop apps waiting for you.

Oh, and if you're the straight-to-the-point type, use the search bar. Want zen vibes? Type "meditation." Craving mental gymnastics? Try "brain games." Dreaming of polyglot status? Search "language learning." Bam! Your options pop up like magic.

And here's the kicker: As you hang out in the App Store, it's like having a buddy who gets you more than your BFF. It learns your tastes from your downloads and clicks, rolling out the red carpet with personalized recommendations in the "Today" and "Apps" sections.

So, whether you're beefing up your phone with cool apps for fitness, brain gains, or just pure fun, the App Store's got your back. Just make sure to do a little window shopping before you commit — check out those app features and any potential price tags. After all, you want your iPhone to be the coolest gadget in town, right?

Let's take a look at some apps that not only enhance your iPhone experience but your life as well.

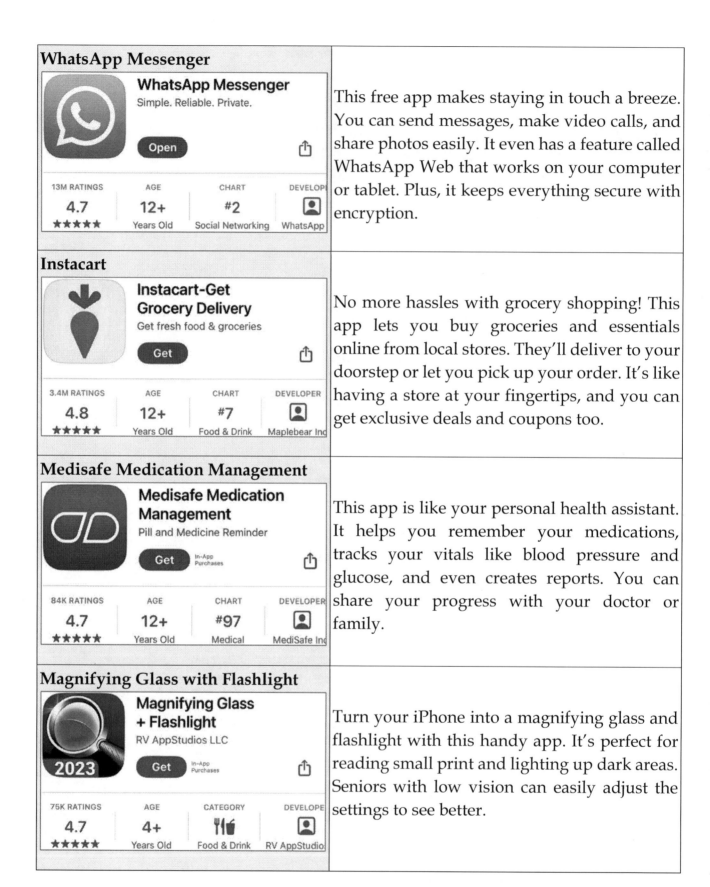

WhatsApp Messenger

This free app makes staying in touch a breeze. You can send messages, make video calls, and share photos easily. It even has a feature called WhatsApp Web that works on your computer or tablet. Plus, it keeps everything secure with encryption.

Instacart

No more hassles with grocery shopping! This app lets you buy groceries and essentials online from local stores. They'll deliver to your doorstep or let you pick up your order. It's like having a store at your fingertips, and you can get exclusive deals and coupons too.

Medisafe Medication Management

This app is like your personal health assistant. It helps you remember your medications, tracks your vitals like blood pressure and glucose, and even creates reports. You can share your progress with your doctor or family.

Magnifying Glass with Flashlight

Turn your iPhone into a magnifying glass and flashlight with this handy app. It's perfect for reading small print and lighting up dark areas. Seniors with low vision can easily adjust the settings to see better.

Impulse Brain Training 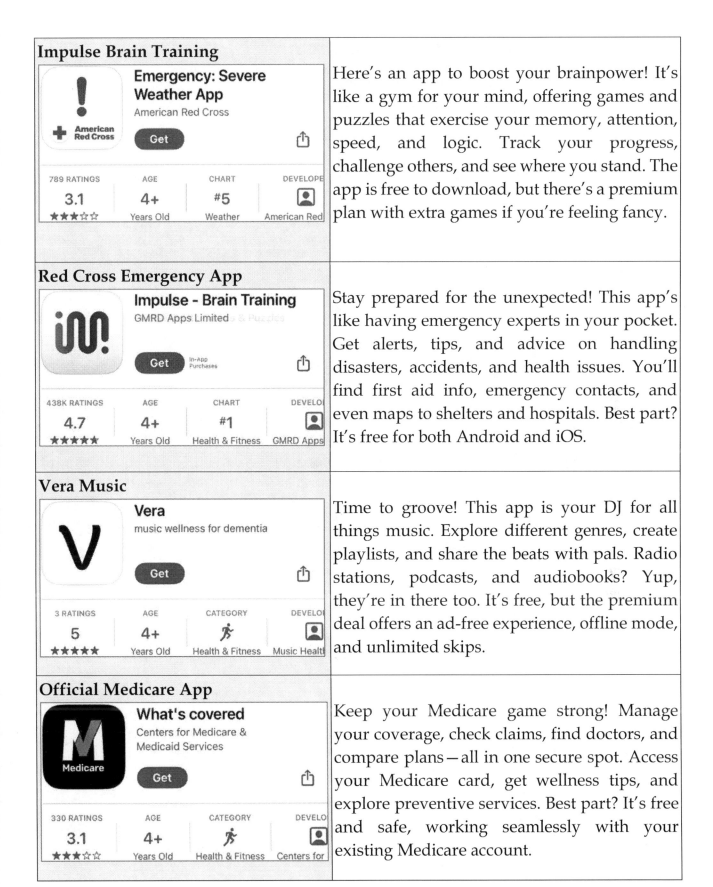 **Emergency: Severe Weather App** American Red Cross Get 789 RATINGS — 3.1 ★★★☆☆ AGE — 4+ Years Old CHART — #5 Weather DEVELOPE — American Red	Here's an app to boost your brainpower! It's like a gym for your mind, offering games and puzzles that exercise your memory, attention, speed, and logic. Track your progress, challenge others, and see where you stand. The app is free to download, but there's a premium plan with extra games if you're feeling fancy.
Red Cross Emergency App **Impulse - Brain Training** GMRD Apps Limited Get — In-App Purchases 438K RATINGS — 4.7 ★★★★★ AGE — 4+ Years Old CHART — #1 Health & Fitness DEVELO — GMRD Apps	Stay prepared for the unexpected! This app's like having emergency experts in your pocket. Get alerts, tips, and advice on handling disasters, accidents, and health issues. You'll find first aid info, emergency contacts, and even maps to shelters and hospitals. Best part? It's free for both Android and iOS.
Vera Music **Vera** music wellness for dementia Get 3 RATINGS — 5 ★★★★★ AGE — 4+ Years Old CATEGORY — 🏃 Health & Fitness DEVELO — Music Health	Time to groove! This app is your DJ for all things music. Explore different genres, create playlists, and share the beats with pals. Radio stations, podcasts, and audiobooks? Yup, they're in there too. It's free, but the premium deal offers an ad-free experience, offline mode, and unlimited skips.
Official Medicare App **What's covered** Centers for Medicare & Medicaid Services Get 330 RATINGS — 3.1 ★★★☆☆ AGE — 4+ Years Old CATEGORY — 🏃 Health & Fitness DEVELO — Centers for	Keep your Medicare game strong! Manage your coverage, check claims, find doctors, and compare plans—all in one secure spot. Access your Medicare card, get wellness tips, and explore preventive services. Best part? It's free and safe, working seamlessly with your existing Medicare account.

Managing your iPhone's apps and documents is essential for maintaining an organized digital space.

- Optimizing storage: Removing unused apps frees up space for other content.

- Enhancing accessibility: Organizing apps ensures quick access to frequently used ones.

- Improving performance: Reducing background processes can speed up your device.

- Personalization: Customizing layouts offers a tailored user experience.

- Security and privacy: Managing app permissions enhances data security.

- Device efficiency: Organizing apps may conserve battery and improve device health.

- User experience: An organized app setup promotes convenience and satisfaction.

By actively managing your apps, you can optimize storage space, streamline functionality, and customize your iPhone experience to better suit your needs, ultimately enhancing your device's performance and usability.

Rearranging Icons

Rearranging icons on your iPhone allows you to personalize the layout for ease of use:

1. Press and Hold

   - Initiating icon movement involves pressing and holding any app icon on your home screen.

   - This action triggers all icons to start "wiggling," indicating they can be rearranged or moved.

2. Drag and Drop

   - While the icons are in the "wiggling" state, drag the desired app icon to your preferred location.

   - You can move it to another screen by navigating to the edges or place it within an existing folder by hovering over the folder.

3. Releasing the Icon

   - Once you've positioned the icon where you want it, release it.

   - This sets the icon in its new location.

This simple process allows you to organize your home screen to suit your preferences, ensuring that the most frequently used apps are easily accessible.

App Folders

App folders are a fantastic way to organize your iPhone's home screen. App folders help categorize and group similar apps together. For instance, you can have a folder for social media apps, another for productivity tools, and so on.

Creating a Folder

1. To create a folder, tap and hold an app icon until it starts to wiggle.

2. Drag one app icon onto another app icon that you want to include in the same folder. This action automatically creates a folder containing both apps.

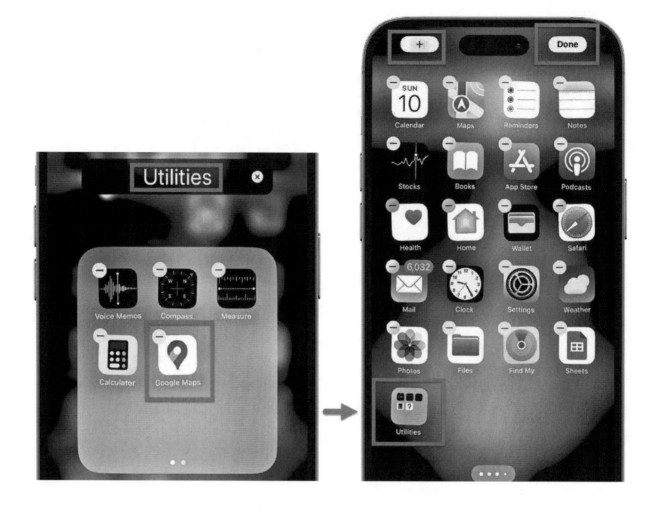

3. Once a folder is created, it can hold multiple apps. You can continue dragging additional app icons into the folder to add them.

To rename the folder, tap on the folder to open it, then tap on the name field. This allows you to rename it as per the category of apps it contains, making it easier to locate. You can also arrange folders on different screens of your iPhone, organizing them according to your preference and making it more convenient to access specific app categories.

Folders make it simpler to reduce clutter on your home screen, as you can have several apps grouped together in a single, easily accessible location. By utilizing folders, you can keep your home screen tidy and efficiently access your apps based on their categories or purposes.

Organizing Documents With the Files App

The Files app is an essential tool for managing documents on your iPhone, acting as a central hub for your files. It consolidates documents stored on your iPhone and those in various cloud services like iCloud Drive, Google Drive, Dropbox, etc., and provides a unified view of your files, allowing easy access and management across different storage platforms.

Managing Documents

1. To organize your documents, open the Files app and tap on "Browse."

2. At the top-right corner, tap the "..." (three dots) icon, then select "New Folder" to create a new folder. You can name this folder based on the documents you plan to store within it.

Moving Documents

After creating folders, you can easily move documents into them.

1. Tap and hold the document you want to move until it starts to wiggle, then select "Move."

2. Choose the destination folder where you want to relocate the document. This action helps maintain a more organized file structure within your storage, making it easier to find specific documents when needed.

By leveraging the Files app, you can efficiently manage and organize your documents, creating a structured system that allows quick access to important files, whether they're stored on your device or in various cloud services.

Uninstalling Apps

There are various reasons that you might want to delete — uninstall — an app.

1. Freeing up space: Apps can occupy a significant amount of storage on your device. Removing less-used or unnecessary apps can free up space for new downloads or updates.

2. Performance improvement: Removing apps can enhance your device's performance, especially if you have many apps running in the background, which can slow down your device.

3. Unused or redundant: Apps that you rarely or never use might clutter your home screen or app library, making it more challenging to find what you need. Deleting these apps declutters your device.

4. Privacy and security: Some apps may pose privacy or security risks. Deleting apps you no longer trust or use can mitigate these risks by reducing potential vulnerabilities.

5. Organizational cleanup: As personal preferences change, organizing the home screen by removing apps that no longer align with your interests or needs can streamline your digital experience.

6. Subscription management: Uninstalling apps that require subscriptions or recurring payments can help manage expenses by eliminating services you no longer wish to pay for.

Ultimately, deleting an app is about managing your device's content, ensuring it aligns with your current needs, preferences, and the available storage on your device.

You can follow these easy steps to remove an app from your phone.

1. Accessing deletion mode

   - Press and hold the app icon on your home screen until the icons start to wiggle. This signifies that you're in deletion mode.

2. Initiating deletion

   - Look for the small "X" symbol that appears on the top left corner (or sometimes top right) of the app icons that are wiggling.

   - Tap on the "X" icon of the app you want to delete.

3. Confirmation

   - A confirmation message or prompt will appear asking if you want to delete the app.

   - Confirm the deletion by selecting "Delete" or "Remove." Some apps may require you to confirm this action with your device's passcode, Touch ID, or Face ID.

4. Completion

   - Once confirmed, the app will be uninstalled, and its icon and associated data will be removed from your device.

Remember, deleting an app removes its data from your device, including any settings or stored information within the app. If it's an app you've purchased and you decide to reinstall it later, you can do so from the App Store without having to repurchase it.

App Updates

Imagine your favorite recipe book. Over time, the author might discover a better way to make your beloved dish or correct a mistake in the recipe. Just like that, apps on your phone regularly receive updates to improve how they work and keep them safe.

Regularly updating apps ensures they run smoothly and you have access to the latest features, similar to keeping your items clean and well-maintained.

- Enhanced performance: Updates often include bug fixes and optimizations that improve app performance, stability, and speed.

- Security patches: Developers regularly release updates to fix security vulnerabilities, ensuring your apps are more secure against potential threats.

- New features: Updates often introduce new functionalities, features, or improvements, enhancing your overall experience with the app.

- Compatibility: Updates ensure that apps remain compatible with the latest operating system versions, preventing compatibility issues.

Updating Apps

1. Accessing updates

   - Open the App Store and tap on the "Updates" tab located at the bottom.

2. Update all or selective updates

   - You have the option to update all apps at once by tapping "Update All" or selectively update specific apps by tapping "Update" next to each app.

3. Automated Process

   - App updates can be set to automatic, ensuring your apps are regularly updated without manual intervention.

Best Practices

1. Set automatic updates

   - Enable automatic updates in your device settings to ensure apps are updated as soon as new versions are available.

2. Frequent check-ins

   - Periodically visit the App Store's update section to manually update any apps that might not have automatically updated.

Maintaining and updating your apps is like performing regular maintenance on your other devices or vehicles. It keeps everything running smoothly and ensures you have access to the latest features and security improvements.

Managing apps, organizing documents, and keeping them up to date enhances your iPhone experience and ensures a well-organized digital environment. Now that you've amassed an array of exciting apps, it's time to share experiences and make the most of your iPhone with your loved ones.

Mid-Book Review Request Page

Opening the Lines of Communication

"When we give cheerfully and accept gratefully, everyone is blessed."
—**Maya Angelou**

I hope you've already been able to put some of what you've learned here into practice. We have more to cover, but before we do, I'd like you to take a moment to think about all the doors that getting to know your iPhone will open for you.

Perhaps you were like my grandmother, and it was selfies that were baffling you… Maybe you were struggling with messaging… Maybe you were getting into frustrated arguments with Siri (trust me, we've all been there!)… Whatever was eluding you, it was keeping you from getting the most out of your device, and in some cases, it may even have been getting in the way of communication with friends and family.

Being able to use your iPhone confidently brings huge peace of mind and enables you to stay connected to your loved ones – and I'm confident that you'll feel your shoulders drop a little when you know that you're certain how to use everything it has to offer without getting stressed out by tech woes that take you by surprise.

I'd hazard a guess that you know other people who could use this advice, so do feel free to share what you've learned with your friends. Information is at its most powerful when we share it. With that in mind, I'd like to ask you a favor. Could you spare a couple of minutes to leave a review so that more people can find this guidance?

By leaving a review of this book on Amazon, you'll show the people who are looking for this information exactly where they can find it.

The older generation doesn't always have the background information that makes it easy to navigate a new device, and sometimes something more is needed than the instructions in the box. Your review will help other people find the guidance they really need to use their iPhone with confidence and enjoy the peace of mind that doing so brings.

Thank you so much for your support. There's no one better placed to help a new reader than someone who's read the information before them.

Please scan the QR code below to leave a review

CHAPTER 6

Virtual Coffee Dates and Social Gatherings: Staying Connected with Loved Ones

People who smile while they are alone used to be called insane until we invented smartphones and social media.
—Mokokoma Mokhonoana

Harnessing the power of your iPhone to maintain connections with loved ones, whether near or far, has never been easier. Embracing avenues like email, video calls, and social media not only bridges distances but also cultivates delightful moments and enduring bonds.

Embracing these digital avenues for communication is a game-changer in maintaining connections

- Email Communication: Email provides a versatile platform for detailed communication. Explore how to compose, send, and manage emails effortlessly on your iPhone, staying connected with lengthy updates and thoughtful messages.

- Video Calls: Dive into the world of video calls using apps like FaceTime or other video messaging platforms available on your iPhone. Discover the joy of seeing loved ones in real-time, regardless of distance.

- Social Media engagement: Explore the world of social media apps on your iPhone, enabling quick updates, sharing moments, and staying in touch with friends and family through posts, messages, and comments.

Utilizing these tools ensures that distance doesn't hinder connections. Whether it's the warmth of an email, the familiarity of a video call, or the constant engagement through social platforms, your iPhone is a gateway to fostering and nurturing those precious connections.

Channeling the Postman: Setting Up and Using Email

The Mail app on your iPhone transforms it into a digital postman, allowing you to send heartfelt messages and share updates in an instant. Just like writing letters but quicker and more immediate, emails keep you connected to family, friends, and the world at large. The Mail app acts as your central hub for managing multiple email accounts seamlessly, making it easier to send, receive, and organize your emails with just a few taps.

Setting Up Your Email Address

Setting up your email on your iPhone is a straightforward process that allows you to access and manage your emails through the Mail app. Here's a detailed breakdown:

1. Accessing the Mail App

   A. Locate the Mail App: Find and tap the "Mail" app icon on your iPhone's home screen. It usually resembles an envelope.

2. Adding a new account

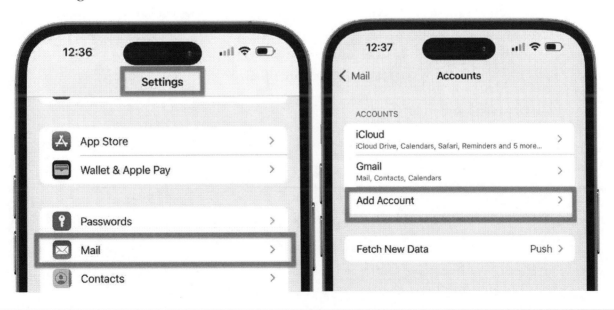

B. Tap "Add Account": Within the Mail app, tap "Add Account." You'll typically find this option in the settings or accounts section.

C. Select your email provider: Choose your email service provider from the list, such as Gmail, Yahoo, Outlook, or others.

3. Entering Credentials

A. Enter your email address and password: Input your email address and associated password in the provided fields.

a) Strong passwords: Use strong passwords and avoid sharing them for email security. Be careful when sharing personal information in emails.

B. Automatic recognition (Optional): For popular email services, the iPhone may automatically recognize settings, simplifying the setup process.

4. Authentication and verification

A. Follow on-screen instructions: Your email provider might require additional authentication steps. Follow any on-screen prompts for verification, which might include security questions or two-factor authentication.

5. Customization (Optional)

A. Adjust sync frequency: You can customize how frequently your iPhone checks for new emails by adjusting the sync frequency settings.

B. Notification preferences: Set up notifications to receive alerts for new emails or tailor them based on your preference for each account.

C. Email signature: Personalize your outgoing emails by creating a custom signature that appears at the end of each email you send. You can include your name, contact information, or a personalized message.

By following these steps, you can seamlessly set up your email account on your iPhone, allowing you to access, send, and manage emails conveniently through the Mail app.

Sending Emails

1. Compose new email

   A. To send an email, open the Mail app and tap the compose icon (usually a pencil or pen icon) to create a new email.

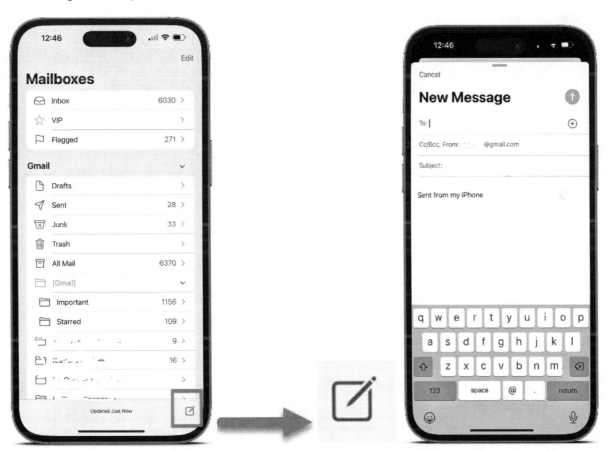

2. Enter the recipient's email address

   A. In the "To" field, enter the email address of the recipient.

3. Compose email

   A. Type your message in the body of the email.

4. Subject line (Optional)

   A. You can add a subject line to summarize the email content.

5. Sending

   A. Once your email is composed, tap "Send" to dispatch it to the recipient.

Receiving and Replying to Emails

1. Inbox access

   A. Open the Mail app to access your inbox. New emails will appear at the top of your inbox.

2. Responding to emails

   B. Tap on the email you wish to respond to.

   C. Tap "Reply" or "Reply All"

   D. Choose "Reply" to respond only to the sender or "Reply All" to reply to all recipients of the email.

3. Compose your response

   A. Type your response in the message field.

4. Send

   A. Once your reply is ready, tap "Send" to send your response.

Saving Attachments and Files

When you receive an email with attachments, tap on the attachment within the email to open and view it directly within the Mail app. This allows you to preview the content of the attachment without downloading it to your device.

Downloading Attachments

To permanently save the attachment to your device for future use:

1. Tap the attachment and look for the "Download" option.

2. Tapping "Download" initiates the saving process, storing the file locally on your iPhone.

Once an attachment has been downloaded, the file is typically stored in the "Downloads" folder within the Mail app. You can access this folder to view and manage the downloaded files.

Additionally, downloaded files can also be accessed through other compatible apps installed on your device. For instance, if it's a PDF, it can be opened with a PDF viewer app, or an image attachment can be found in your Photos app.

Managing attachments and files efficiently within the Mail app enables easy access to important documents, photos, or other content received through emails on your iPhone.

Organizing and Managing Emails

In the Mail app, creating custom folders can help you efficiently sort and organize your emails based on different categories or priorities.

Creating Custom Folders

1. Open the Mail app on your iPhone.

2. Tap "Mailboxes" located at the top-left or bottom-left corner of the screen.

3. Tap "Edit" and then "New Mailbox" to create a new folder.

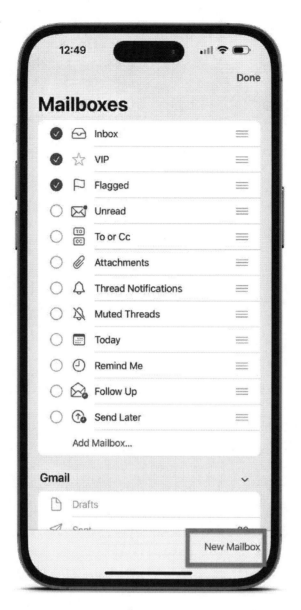

4. Enter a name for the folder (e.g., "Work," "Personal," "Travel," etc.).

5. Select the location where you want to place the folder (e.g., "Mailbox" or an existing account).

6. Tap "Save" or "Done" to create the folder

Enhancing User-Friendliness

To enhance readability, adjust the font sizes in your iPhone settings. Navigate to the Settings 🔘 app > Display & Brightness > Text Size to choose a larger font for easier reading of emails.

1. Go to the Settings ⊚ app on your iPhone.

2. Scroll down and select "Display & Brightness."

3. Tap on "Text Size."

4. Use the slider to adjust the font size to your preference. Move it towards the right for larger text.

5. Exit the Settings; the changes will be applied system-wide, including the Mail app.

For hands-free convenience, utilize Siri by saying, "Hey Siri, read my emails," to have your emails read aloud, providing an alternative way to access and engage with your messages.

1. Activate Siri by saying "Hey Siri" or holding the Side or Home button, depending on your iPhone model.

2. Once Siri is activated, say, "Read my emails."

3. Siri will begin reading your latest unread emails aloud.

Managing Mailboxes and Folders

Use the Mail app's folder feature to organize your emails effectively. Create distinct folders to categorize emails based on topics or importance, providing easier access and management.

1. Creating folders

   - Follow steps similar to creating custom folders mentioned earlier within the Mail app.

2. Renaming or deleting folders

   A. Open the Mail app and navigate to the "Mailboxes" section.

   B. Tap "Edit."

   C. Select the folder you want to rename or delete.

   D. To rename, tap on the folder's name, edit it, and tap "Done"

   E. To delete, tap "Delete Mailbox" and confirm the action.

In the Mail app, you can easily manage these folders by creating new ones, renaming existing folders, or deleting unnecessary ones to streamline your email organization process.

Moving Emails to Junk or Blocking Senders

To declutter your inbox of unwanted emails, mark them as junk by tapping the flag icon and selecting "Move to Junk." This action helps in identifying and removing spam or irrelevant emails.

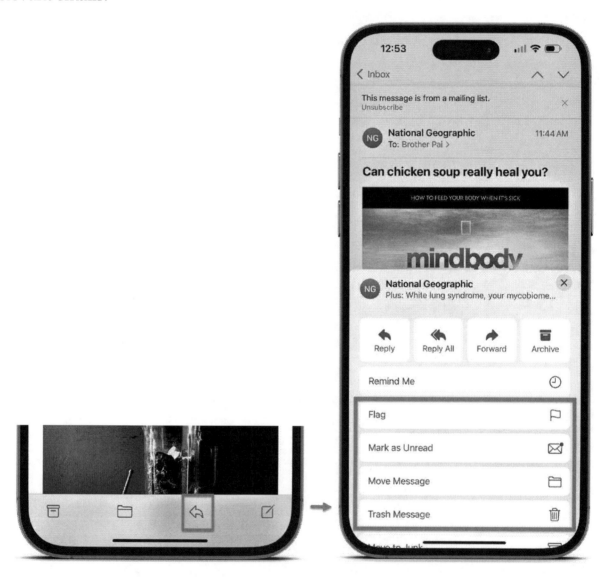

Moving Emails to Junk

1. Open the Mail app and locate the email you want to mark as junk.

2. Tap the email to open it.

3. Tap the flag icon at the bottom.

4. Select "Move to Junk" to move the email to the Junk folder.

Additionally, if you wish to prevent specific senders from contacting you, block them by tapping on their email address and choosing "Block this Contact" or "Block this Sender." This feature helps in managing and controlling your incoming emails effectively.

Blocking Senders

1. Open the Mail app and locate an email from the sender you want to block.

2. Tap on the sender's email address.

3. Tap "Block this Contact" or "Block this Sender" to prevent further emails from that sender.

Performing these steps will help you effectively manage your emails, folders, and settings within the Mail app on your iPhone.

Senior-Friendly Email Apps

Consider exploring alternative email provider apps tailored towards your needs for a more user-friendly experience. These apps often simplify the interface for easier navigation and usage.

1. Airmail

   - Airmail is known for its clean and customizable interface.

   - It supports multiple email accounts and allows customization of swipe gestures for easier navigation.

   - Offers various themes and allows font customization for better readability.

2. Edison Mail

- Known for its simplicity and user-friendly design.

- Features a Smart Assistant that organizes emails into categories like subscriptions, travel, packages, and bills.

- Offers an undo send feature and has a built-in block sender option.

3. ProtonMail

- Focuses on security and privacy with end-to-end encryption.

- Offers a simple and intuitive interface with large buttons and clear fonts.

- Provides easy-to-use tools for managing emails and contacts.

4. Gmail (Google Mail)

- Known for its widespread use and familiarity.

- Provides an accessible interface and offers various customization options.

- Features like conversation view and smart folders can streamline email management.

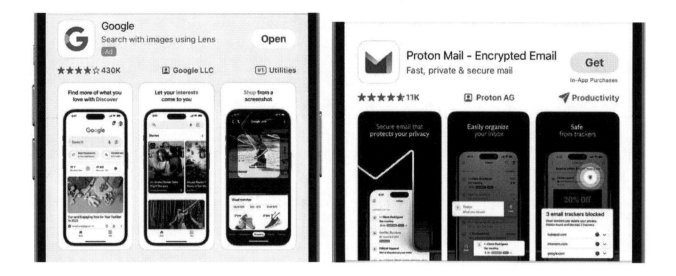

5. Yahoo Mail

- Offers a user-friendly interface with customizable themes.

- Features a powerful search function and easy organization of emails into folders.

- Provides a calendar, news, and other functionalities within the app.

These email apps often offer features such as larger fonts, simplified navigation, intuitive layouts, and sometimes voice-activated commands, catering to seniors or individuals looking for a more straightforward email experience. Exploring these apps might help you find one that aligns best with your preferences and needs.

Face-to-Face Anywhere: Making the Most of FaceTime

Through video calls, your iPhone transforms into a portal connecting faces and hearts across miles. Whether it's a virtual coffee date with a friend or a family reunion through the screen, seeing and hearing loved ones fosters a sense of togetherness.

FaceTime offers a seamless video calling experience, bridging distances for face-to-face conversations much like being in the same room. It's akin to having that coffee date with your best friend or sharing bedtime stories with your grandchild, irrespective of the physical miles between you.

Initiating a FaceTime call is a breeze. Similar to making a regular call, you can start a FaceTime call by simply locating the person you wish to call in your contacts and tapping the FaceTime button. Plus, since FaceTime uses Wi-Fi, it doesn't consume your phone plan's minutes.

When engaging in a FaceTime call, remember to look directly at the camera — the small dot at the top of your screen. This simple action allows the other person to feel as if you're looking at them directly.

Here's how to start a FaceTime call

1. Access FaceTime > Open the "Contacts" app on your iPhone

2. Select contact > Choose the contact you want to FaceTime with by scrolling or using the search bar.

3. Initiate FaceTime

   A. Once you've selected the contact, tap the "FaceTime" icon (it looks like a video camera) next to their name.

4. Wait for connection

   A. FaceTime will attempt to connect to the other person. They'll receive a notification that you're trying to FaceTime with them.

5. Accept the call

   A. If the other person accepts your FaceTime call, you'll see their video feed, and they'll see yours if your camera is enabled. You're now on a FaceTime call!

6. End the call

   A. To end the FaceTime call, tap the red "End" button at the bottom center of the screen.

Remember, for FaceTime to work, both you and the person you're calling need to have FaceTime enabled on your devices and have an internet connection — Wi-Fi or cellular data.

While other options exist for video calling services, FaceTime stands out as an inbuilt iOS feature, ensuring compatibility and seamless integration with your iPhone. Give it a try — it's a fantastic way to bring the personal touch of face-to-face conversations right to your device.

Joining the Party: Understanding and Using Social Media Apps

Engaging on social media through your iPhone is like curating a digital scrapbook of life's moments — a space where memories are captured and connections flourish. It's a platform where laughter, photos, and stories transcend physical distances, fostering a sense of togetherness.

In the digital age, smartphones and social media redefine companionship. Being alone doesn't imply isolation; it's an era of shared smiles, echoing laughter, and heartfelt connections through screens.

Your iPhone serves as a bridge to these connections, transforming every interaction into a cherished moment. Social media apps like Facebook and Instagram create a perpetual gathering — a virtual space where friendships thrive and familial bonds stay alive.

To begin this digital journey, download these apps from the App Store, follow the setup instructions, and ensure your account's security with a robust password. Customize your profile and privacy settings on Facebook to control your information visibility, and remember to exercise caution with personal details while maintaining respectful interactions.

Facebook: Connecting People and Communities

Facebook is a popular social networking platform that allows users to connect with friends, family, and communities worldwide. It serves as a digital space for sharing moments, thoughts, and interests through posts, photos, and videos.

Downloading Facebook

1. Access the App Store - Open the App Store on your iPhone. You can find it on your home screen with the blue icon featuring an "A."

2. Search for Facebook - Tap on the search bar at the bottom of the App Store and type "Facebook" into the search field.

3. Download the App - Once you find the official Facebook app, tap on it. Then tap "Get" or the cloud icon with a down arrow to start the download.

4. Install the App - After downloading, the app will automatically install on your iPhone. You can find it on your home screen, simply tap on the app icon to open it.

Setting Up Your Account

1. **Creating an account** - Open the Facebook app and follow the on-screen instructions to create your account. This involves entering your name, email, or phone number, creating a password, and adding some basic personal information.

2. **Security measures** - Ensure your account security by setting a strong password and refraining from sharing it with anyone. This helps protect your account from unauthorized access.

Customize your privacy settings in the app to control who can view your posts and personal information. Always remember to avoid sharing sensitive details publicly and maintain respectful interactions with others. Remember, anything you post can be seen by your connections, so be mindful of the content you share.

Once your account is set up, start connecting with friends and family by sending friend requests. Like or comment on posts from your connections. Share your own photos, thoughts, and experiences. Join groups based on your interests to engage with like-minded individuals.

Remember, Facebook is a space for connecting and sharing, so be mindful of what you post, ensuring it aligns with your comfort level of sharing personal information with your connected network.

Instagram: A Visual Storytelling Platform

Instagram offers a visually engaging platform where you can like, comment, and share posts, emphasizing visual content for a unique social experience. Dive into this digital realm, connect with loved ones, and explore the myriad joys of social media on your iPhone.

Downloading Instagram

Access the App Store: Open the App Store on your iPhone.

Search for Instagram: Tap the search bar at the bottom of the App Store, type "Instagram" in the search field, and look for the official Instagram app.

Download and Install: Tap on the Instagram app, then tap "Get" or the cloud icon to download the app. Once downloaded, it will automatically install on your iPhone.

Open the App: Find the Instagram icon on your home screen and tap on it to open the app.

Creating an Account

1. **Account setup** - To create an account, open the Instagram app and tap "Sign Up." Enter your email address or phone number, create a username and password, and add a profile picture.

2. **Profile information** - Customize your profile by adding a bio, profile picture, and any personal information you feel comfortable sharing.

3. **Strong Password** - Ensure your account security by creating a strong password unique to your Instagram account.

4. **Account privacy** - Adjust your privacy settings to control who can see your posts and who can follow you. Decide if you want a public or private account.

5. **Content Sharing** - Remember that anything you post can be viewed by your followers, so be cautious about sharing sensitive personal information.

Engaging on Instagram

1. **Follow people** - Start by following friends, family, celebrities, or accounts related to your interests. Tap the magnifying glass icon to search for users or content.

2. **Engage with Posts** - Like, comment, or share posts from your connections. You can also send direct messages to communicate privately.

3. **Explore features** - Use Instagram Stories to share temporary photos or videos. Discover new content through the Explore tab, where you can find posts and accounts tailored to your interests.

Instagram thrives on visual storytelling and community engagement, offering a platform to showcase your interests, hobbies, and experiences through captivating visuals.

As Mokokoma Mokhonoana wisely remarked, the digital realm has redefined the norm. With smartphones and social media, being alone doesn't equate to isolation. It's an era where smiles are shared, laughs echo through screens, and hearts connect despite physical distances.

In the digital landscape, your iPhone is a conduit for human connections, making every interaction a shared moment worth cherishing.

CHAPTER 7

Safeguarding Your Digital Life: iPhone's Security and Privacy Features Uncovered

You know something is wrong when the government declares opening someone else's mail is a felony but your internet activity is fair game for data collecting.
—E.A. Bucchianeri

Your iPhone isn't just a device; it's a gateway to your digital life. It holds personal information, communicates sensitive data, and connects you with the world. Understanding its security and privacy features is crucial in safeguarding your digital footprint.

Your iPhone comes equipped with various security and privacy features to protect your data:

- Passcode & Face/Touch ID: Set a passcode, Face ID, or Touch ID to secure access to your device. This prevents unauthorized users from accessing your personal information.

- App permissions: Manage app permissions to control which apps have access to features like location, camera, microphone, and contacts. This ensures your data isn't accessed without your consent.

- Find My iPhone: Activate "Find My iPhone" to track your device if lost and remotely lock or erase its data if necessary. It's a powerful tool to protect your information in case of theft or misplacement.

- Two-Factor Authentication (2FA): Enable 2FA for added security on your Apple ID and other accounts. This adds an extra layer of protection by requiring a verification code along with your password.

- Privacy Settings: Explore the Privacy settings to manage how your data is used by Apple and third-party apps. Adjust settings to limit tracking, personalize ad experiences, and control data shared with apps.

- Secure Enclave & Encryption: Benefit from the device's secure enclave and encryption, safeguarding your personal data stored on the device from unauthorized access.

Understanding and utilizing these features ensures your iPhone remains a fortress for your personal data, maintaining your digital security and privacy. Regularly updating your device and being cautious about the apps you install further bolsters these defenses.

Protect Your Phone: Setting Up Passcodes and Face ID

Your iPhone's passcode acts as a guardian for your personal information. It's the initial barricade against unwanted access to your emails, messages, and other sensitive data. A passcode prevents someone from casually browsing through your iPhone's contents without your consent, ensuring your privacy.

If your iPhone gets misplaced or stolen, a passcode acts as a barrier, preventing unauthorized access to your personal data and minimizing the risk of identity theft.

Setting a Secure Passcode

Usually, a four- or six-digit passcode is required but longer passcodes or an alphanumeric code can significantly bolster your device's security. Let's have a look at how you can set up an easy-to-remember passcode that is still secure.

1. Open the "Settings" 🎛 app on your iPhone's home screen with a tap.

2. Select "Face ID & Passcode" or "Touch ID & Passcode" (Note: Depending on your iPhone model and settings, you might see either of these options. Tap on it.)

3. Enter current passcode (if applicable)

A. If you've already set up a passcode and want to change it, you'll be prompted to enter your current passcode first.

4. Set a new passcode.

A. Tap "Turn Passcode On" or "Change Passcode."

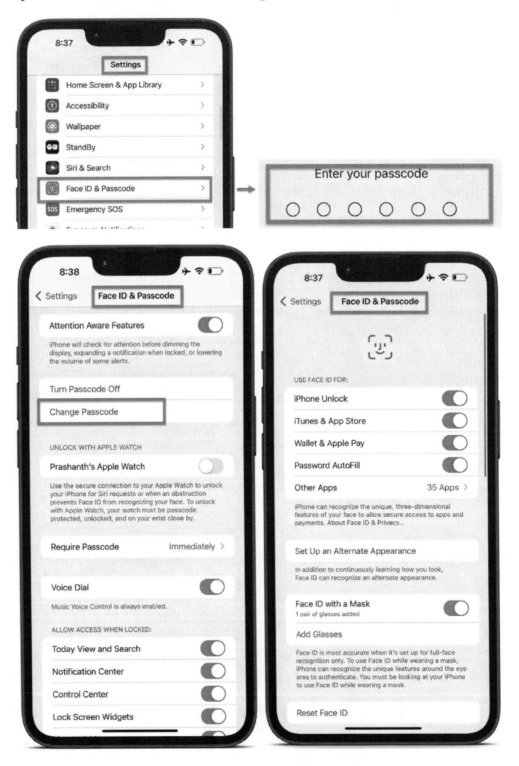

5. Enter a new passcode.

   A. Follow the prompts to enter a new passcode. You can choose a 4-digit numeric code by default, but for increased security, tap "Passcode Options" to select a Custom Numeric Code or Custom Alphanumeric Code.

   B. If choosing a custom passcode, enter your new passcode as prompted, whether it's a longer numeric code or an alphanumeric code containing letters and numbers.

   C. Create a secure passcode that's easy to remember like using a memorable phrase or sequence. For instance, consider the phrase "I love gardening in 2023!" You can convert this phrase into a secure passcode by using the first letters of each word and adding some numbers and symbols, for example, ILGi2023! This passcode incorporates the first letters of each word, combines uppercase and lowercase letters, includes numbers, and ends with a symbol to enhance security. It's memorable yet complex enough to provide good security for your phone.

6. Confirm the New Passcode

   A. You'll be asked to enter the new passcode again to confirm it.

7. Verify Face ID or Touch ID (if applicable)

   A. If you're setting up a new device or using Face ID or Touch ID for the first time, follow the on-screen instructions to enroll your face or fingerprint for biometric authentication. We'll have a deeper look at Face ID in the next section.

8. Passcode Set

   A. Once completed, your new passcode is set up and active.

Remember, it's crucial to keep your passcode secure and not share it with anyone to maintain the privacy and security of your device and data.

Adopting Biometric Authentication (Face ID)

Face ID serves as a convenient and secure alternative, using facial recognition technology unique to each user. This method replaces the need for remembering complex codes and offers robust protection.

Setting Up Face ID

1. Launch the "Settings" app on your iPhone's home screen

2. Scroll down and tap on "Face ID & Passcode." If prompted, enter your existing passcode.

3. Within the Face ID & Passcode settings, tap on "Set Up Face ID." This initiates the setup process.

4. Scan your face

   A. Follow the on-screen instructions.

   B. Position your face within the frame provided and ensure it's adequately visible.

   C. Tilt your head slightly and move it in a circular motion as the iPhone guides you.

   D. Ensure your face remains entirely within the frame during this process.

5. Finish setup

   A. Once the scan completes, the device will notify you that Face ID has been successfully set up.

   B. You can proceed by tapping "Done" or following any additional prompts.

Here are some tips for the optimal Face ID Setup.

1. Good lighting

   Ensure you're in a well-lit area during setup. Avoid extreme lighting conditions or direct sunlight on your face.

2. Positioning

   Hold the device at a comfortable distance (around 10-20 inches away) and maintain a natural angle when positioning your face within the frame.

3. Full face coverage

   Make sure your entire face, including the edges, is captured during the scanning process.

After setting up Face ID, it can be used for various functions such as unlocking your iPhone, authorizing app purchases, or logging into apps that support Face ID authentication.

Face ID can be a convenient and secure way to access your device, but having a backup passcode is advisable in case Face ID isn't available or in situations where it may not work optimally.

Using Face ID

1. Unlocking your iPhone

    A. Simply pick up your iPhone and glance at the screen.

    B. If Face ID recognizes you, the lock icon will animate, indicating that the phone has been unlocked.

    C. Swipe up from the bottom of the screen or tap the screen to access the Home screen.

2. App authentication

    A. Face ID can be utilized for various in-app authentications that support facial recognition.

    B. For instance, when making App Store purchases, downloading apps, or using secure apps like banking or password managers, Face ID can authorize these actions.

    C. When prompted, glance at your device to allow the authentication process to complete.

While Face ID is secure, it's advisable to have a backup passcode set up, as we discussed in the previous section, in case Face ID fails or as an alternative authentication method.

Strengthening Overall Security

To strengthen the overall security of your phone, let's have a look at the auto-lock feature and data encryption. While these measures bolster security, it's important to find a balance that doesn't hinder your experience significantly.

Auto-Lock Feature

Auto-lock is a setting on your iPhone that controls how long the device remains active before it locks itself and goes into sleep mode when not in use. It's a security feature that helps protect your phone from unauthorized access if it's left unattended.

When you set a shorter auto-lock duration, your iPhone will automatically lock itself faster after a period of inactivity. For instance, if you set it to lock after 30 seconds of no interaction, the screen will turn off and require authentication (Face ID, passcode, or Touch ID) to be accessed again.

To adjust this setting:

- Go to the "Settings" app > Tap "Display & Brightness." > Select "Auto-Lock" and set a shorter duration (like 30 seconds or a minute).

This ensures that if the device is left unattended, it locks itself swiftly, reducing the window of opportunity for unauthorized access.

Data Encryption

Data encryption is a security method that converts information stored on your iPhone into an unreadable format. This encryption process uses complex algorithms to encode data, making it indecipherable without the correct decryption key (typically your passcode or Face ID).

When you enable device encryption on your iPhone, all the data stored on the device, including personal information, files, app data, and settings, gets scrambled into an encrypted format. Even if someone gains unauthorized access to your device or tries to retrieve the data without proper authorization, the information will be unreadable and inaccessible without the correct decryption key.

To enable device encryption:

- Navigate to the "Settings" app > Select "Face ID & Passcode" > Tap on "Data Protection."

Once enabled, the iPhone encrypts all stored data, ensuring that even if someone gains unauthorized access to the device, the data remains protected and unreadable without the correct passcode or Face ID authentication.

Enabling device encryption ensures that if your iPhone falls into the wrong hands, the sensitive information stored within remains protected. This feature significantly enhances the overall security of your device by safeguarding your personal data from unauthorized access or breaches.

The Privacy Shield: Managing Your iPhone's Privacy Settings

Privacy settings on your iPhone dictate which applications have access to your personal information and location data. Managing these settings empowers you to regulate what information gets shared and with whom, enhancing your control over your digital footprint and safeguarding your privacy.

Your iPhone's privacy settings are like the bouncers at a club—they decide which apps get access to your personal info and location. Taking charge of these settings is your VIP pass to control who gets what, boosting your digital safety.

Some insider tips to keep your iPhone fortress secure:

Watch out for sneaky apps. Stick to trusted spots like the App Store to dodge those shady characters trying to steal your data or mess up your device.

Malware? Nah. Be wary of random links or downloads, especially from unknown sources—they could be hiding trouble.

App permissions: Don't hand out VIP access unless it is absolutely necessary. Review what each app wants and only dish out the data it really needs to function.

Public Wi-Fi is like a crowded street—be careful what you share. Stick to secure networks with passwords to keep your private stuff private.

Passwords are the gatekeepers to your accounts. Weak ones or using the same key for all doors? Not cool. Go for unique, strong passwords, or try a password manager for a master key.

Your iPhone's security game is top-notch! With every new model, Apple beefs up its defenses with fancy tech and encryption. Your data is in a fortress, guarded against sneaky intruders, thanks to these smart moves by Apple.

Managing App Privacy Settings

Let's talk app privacy — it's like being the bouncer at a VIP party, deciding who gets the backstage pass to your personal data. Yep, you're the boss!

You've got the power to control what these apps peek at, like contacts, locations, photos, and even your mic — no sneak peeks without your say-so!

Why is this gig important? Well, you're the guardian of your data kingdom, protecting it from those pesky apps that might misuse or snoop around where they shouldn't.

To play the privacy game like a pro:

1. Get to the settings party: Open "Settings" app on your iPhone and hunt down "Privacy."

2. Data types, AKA the guest list: There's a whole list of VIP data types — Contacts, Location Services, Photos, Camera, Mic, and more. Each one's a piece of your kingdom that apps might want to peek at.

3. Gatekeeping time: Tap into a data type like "Location Services" to see which apps are begging for a backstage pass to your whereabouts.

4. Flex that control: Play God by toggling switches. Want to keep an app out of your location club? Just flick its switch off.

Now, here's the pro move — do a regular sweep! Check these settings now and then, especially after installing new apps or when your phone gets a makeover. It's like checking your house for surprise guests — keep that control tight!

By being the gatekeeper of your data, you're a privacy pro. You control what these apps get to see, keeping your kingdom safe from shady characters trying to sneak a peek.

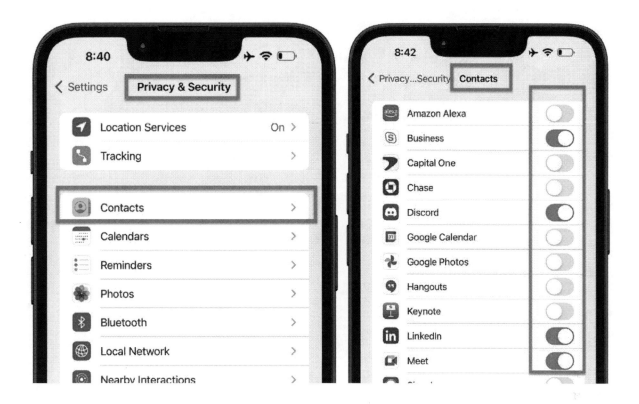

Outsmarting the Scammers: Avoiding Scams and Protecting Personal Information

Phishing scams: It's like fishing for your personal info, but way less relaxing. These are sneaky attempts to try to snag stuff like your usernames, passwords, credit card details — basically, anything they can get their virtual hands on.

Picture this: An email or text pops up, looking all official. It's like a wolf in sheep's clothing, pretending to be from a trustworthy source. But hold up, here's how to spot these troublemakers:

1. Watch those email details: Check the sender's address closely. Phishing emails might look legit, but they'll often have wonky or misspelled domains. For instance, that "bank" email might come from a URL that's just a bit off from the real deal.

2. No free lunches or urgent demands: If they're dangling prizes or begging for urgent info, think twice. Scammers love to bait you with freebies or scare you into clicking suspicious links that take you to their trickster websites.

3. Distrust unsolicited requests: Did you get a call or message out of the blue asking for sensitive stuff? Red flag! Always double-check who's asking before giving away the keys to your castle. If it feels fishy, it probably is.

4. Click wariness: Hover over links before clicking. Check where they're really taking you. And don't go punching in your info on sites that seem sketchy or aren't locked down tight.

Stay sharp, stay safe! By playing detective with suspicious messages and requests, you're putting up a fortress around your personal info, keeping those virtual fishers at bay.

Browsing the Web Safely

Browsing the web safely on your iPhone? Safari has got your back with a cool feature called the Privacy Report. It's like your digital detective, showing who's trying to track your moves online.

Here's how to summon this superpower:

1. Safari Summoning: Open Safari, the trusty browser on your iPhone.

2. Icon Exploration: Look up the top-left for the "AA" icon—it's your portal to privacy.

3. Privacy Peek: Tap on it and choose "Privacy Report" from the dropdown menu.

4. Detective Work: Now, you're in the spy zone! Check out how many trackers got the boot, which ones got a pass, and which sneaky websites they're from.

It's like Safari's your bodyguard, blocking those nosy trackers from peeking into your online moves. Keep an eye on that report to see who's trying to snoop and who got blocked at the door!

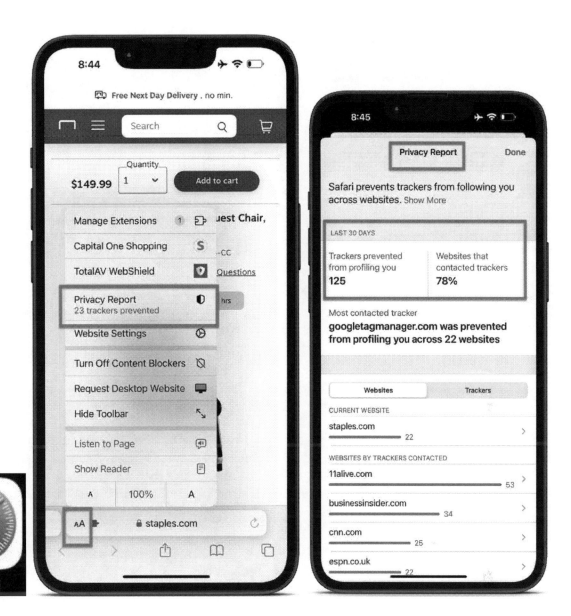

Fraudulent Website Warning

Activate this feature in Safari settings to receive alerts when you stumble upon suspected phishing sites. This proactive warning system helps you steer clear of potentially harmful websites.

1. Go to the Settings ⚙ app on your iPhone.

2. Scroll down and locate "Safari" from the list of apps in Settings.

3. Enable **Fraudulent Website Warning**

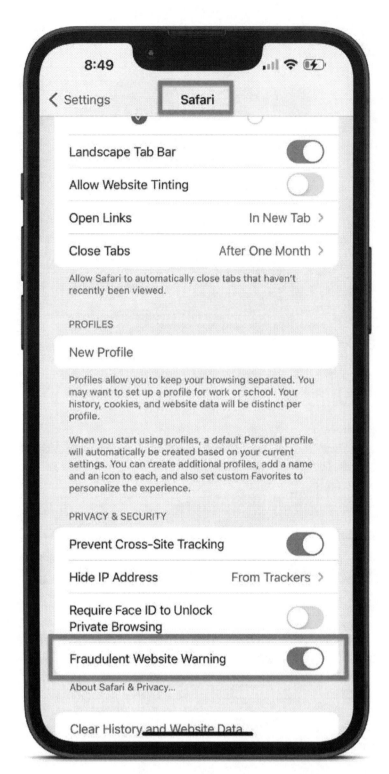

- Inside Safari settings, locate "Fraudulent Website Warning" and toggle it on.

- This feature will now alert you if Safari suspects that a website, you're visiting is potentially fraudulent or a phishing site.

By utilizing Safari's Privacy Report and enabling the Fraudulent Website Warning, you're empowering yourself with tools to protect your privacy and avoid potentially harmful websites while browsing on your iPhone.

App downloads from the App Store

Stick to downloading apps exclusively from the App Store. Apple meticulously vets all apps before they are available, ensuring they are free from malicious software or any harmful elements that could compromise your device's security.

Built-in privacy and security features

Utilize the inherent security features of your iPhone, such as device encryption, robust passcodes, or Face ID authentication. Manage app permission settings to control access to your data, adding an extra layer of security.

Phishing awareness

Be vigilant and cautious of suspicious messages or emails asking for personal information or containing links to unknown sites. Avoid interacting with such content to shield yourself from potential phishing attempts.

By employing these tools and exercising caution while navigating the online world, you can create a safer and more secure digital experience on your iPhone. This ensures a protected browsing environment while maintaining your privacy and security.

Now that you have explored securing your digital world, let's shift our focus to tailoring your iPhone to your specific needs.

CHAPTER 8

Tailoring Your iPhone to Your Needs

For a total of 36 seconds, Schiller spoke somewhat awkwardly about VoiceOver, Zoom, White on Black (called Invert Colors from iOS 6 onward), and Mono Audio – the first real accessibility features on the iPhone OS platform, as it was then called.
— Shelly Brisbin

Before we continue on our journey of iPhone discovery, here's a little fun fact; iOS's accessibility features are a testament to Apple's dedication to enhancing usability and inclusivity. Apple's dedication to accessibility has been transformative. It's incredible to witness how a simple 36-second demo has evolved into an extensive array of features that cater to diverse user needs, emphasizing inclusivity and usability.

The journey began with VoiceOver in 2009, marking a monumental step toward making the iPhone more accessible to individuals with visual impairments. This groundbreaking screen reader paved the way for a whole suite of accessibility tools. Apple's commitment didn't stop there; it continued expanding these features, earning commendations for prioritizing technology that's inclusive for all.

In this chapter, we'll explore the depth of accessibility options on your iPhone. It's not merely about making calls or staying connected through social media; your iPhone offers a wealth of functionalities catering to various needs. So, let's delve into the vast array of accessibility features available and unlock the true potential of your iPhone for every user.

The iPhone's settings to enhance visibility and accessibility can significantly improve your user experience, especially for individuals with visual impairments. In this section you'll find a detailed guide that dives into essential adjustments within Display & Brightness and Display & Text Size settings, empowering you to tailor your screen brightness and enlarge text for better readability across your device. Moreover, exploring the Magnifier tool in Accessibility settings opens up a world of close-up clarity, leveraging your iPhone's camera as a magnifying glass to zoom in on small prints or objects effortlessly.

Follow these step-by-step instructions to make your iPhone's display more comfortable and accommodating to your visual needs, ensuring a smoother and more accessible journey through your device.

Brightness Adjustment

I'm sure you've had those moments where your screen brightness is just too much but then you go outside and you can't see a darn thing on your phone. Don't worry, there is a quick and easy solution.

1. Unlock your iPhone and locate the "Settings" 🔘 app > Scroll down to Display & Brightness and tap on "Display & Brightness."

2. Adjust Brightness

   A. In the Display & Brightness settings, you'll find a brightness slider at the top of the screen.

   B. Slide the brightness bar to the right to increase the screen brightness or to the left to decrease it.

   C. As you adjust, the screen brightness will change, allowing you to find a comfortable level suitable for your visibility in different lighting environments.

   D. Test it out in various settings to ensure optimal readability and comfort.

3. Automatic brightness (optional)

   A. To enable Automatic Brightness, toggle the switch next to "Auto-Brightness."

B. This feature adjusts your screen's brightness based on ambient light conditions, offering convenience and preserving battery life.

By following these steps, you can effortlessly adjust your iPhone's brightness to suit your preferences and ensure comfortable visibility in different lighting environments.

Text Enlargement

Adjusting text size sure stands out, particularly for those seeking enhanced readability and accessibility. This feature allows you to tailor your device's interface to match your visual preferences and requirements. By exploring the steps to enlarge text within the Display & Text Size settings, you can have a clearer and more comfortable viewing experience, making every interaction with your iPhone more accessible and user-friendly.

1. Unlock your iPhone and locate the "Settings" 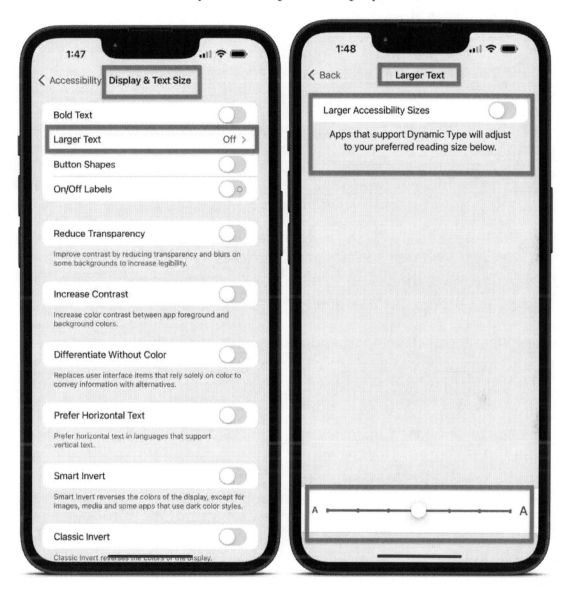 app > Scroll down and select "Accessibility."

2. Navigate to Display & Text Size

   A. Within the Accessibility menu, tap on "Display & Text Size."

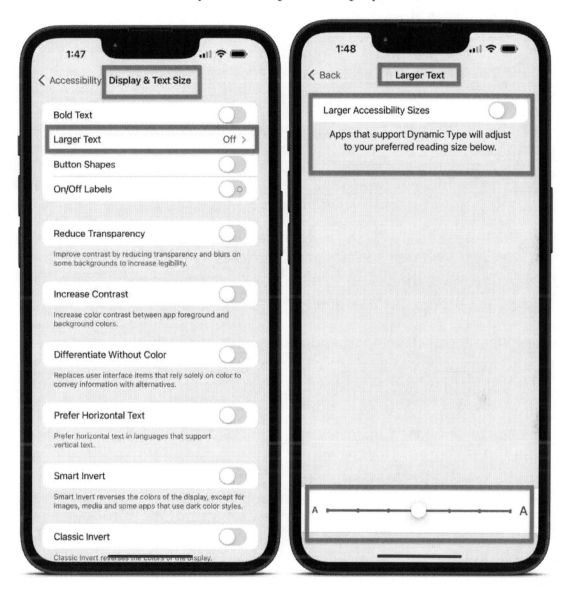

3. Adjust text size

   A. Toggle on "Larger Text" by tapping the switch next to it.

   B. Using the slider below, adjust the text size according to your preference.

   C. When you toggle on Larger Text, additional sliders will appear, allowing you to set a custom text size beyond the standard options.

4. Custom text size (Optional)

   A. You can fine-tune the text size by using the additional sliders that appear when you enable "Larger Text."

   B. Adjust the text size using these sliders until you find a size that is comfortable and easy to read for you.

By following these steps, you can easily increase the text size on your iPhone, ensuring that messages, labels, and content across the device are more visible and accessible to you.

Magnifier Tool

The Magnifier feature on the iPhone is designed to offer a convenient and user-friendly way to magnify objects or texts in your surroundings. Accessible via the Accessibility settings, enabling this tool grants quick access to a magnifying glass-like function using the device's camera. Upon activation, you can triple-press the Side Button (for Face ID-enabled iPhones) to open the Magnifier swiftly. This opens the device's camera interface, providing a zoom slider at the bottom for seamless magnification control.

Once in the Magnifier, you are able to adjust the zoom level by sliding your finger along the slider, zooming in or out as needed. To freeze the image for a closer examination, tapping the round capture button in the middle of the screen proves helpful. Additionally, there's an option to refine the image further by adjusting brightness and contrast settings through the filter icon, optimizing the viewing experience.

1. Open your iPhone and locate the "Settings" app > Scroll down and tap on "Accessibility."

2. In the Accessibility menu, find and select "Magnifier." Toggle on the Magnifier option to activate the magnifier feature

3. Using the Magnifier

   A. To quickly access the Magnifier, triple-press the Side Button (for iPhones with Face ID).

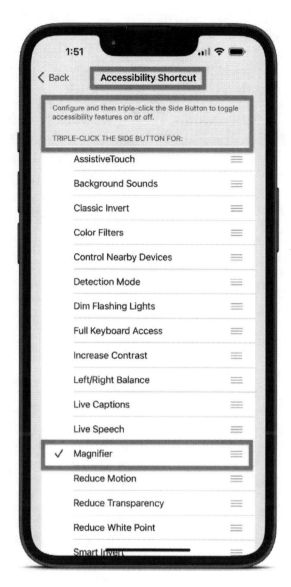

B. The camera will open up, and you can now use the slider at the bottom to zoom in and out.

C. Tap the round button in the middle to freeze the image for a closer look.

Adjust brightness and contrast by tapping the filter icon for a clearer view.

This tool serves as a valuable asset, especially for those with visual impairments or anyone requiring a closer look at small text, fine details, or objects.

Enhancing accessibility is a priority within iOS, offering a suite of features catering to diverse hearing needs. From seamless connections with hearing aids to visual alerts and nuanced audio adjustments, iOS ensures a more inclusive experience for users with varying hearing abilities. These functionalities aim to provide clarity, convenience, and tailored experiences, ensuring everyone can engage with their devices comfortably and effectively.

Hearing Devices Connectivity

Hearing device settings facilitate seamless connections between hearing aids and the iPhone. This integration enables individuals to experience clearer and amplified sound, customized to their unique hearing requirements.

Before you connect your hearing aids to your phone, first we need to make sure the Bluetooth is turned on.

1. Unlock your iPhone and go to the home screen > Locate and tap on the "Settings" app.

2. In the Settings menu, scroll down to find and select "Bluetooth." Open Bluetooth Settings.

3. Enable Bluetooth

   A. On the Bluetooth screen, you'll see a toggle switch at the top.

   B. Tap the toggle switch to turn on Bluetooth; it will appear green when activated.

4. Pairing Devices

   A. Once Bluetooth is enabled, your iPhone will start searching for nearby Bluetooth devices.

   B. To pair a specific device (like hearing aids, headphones, or other accessories), ensure the device is in pairing mode and select it from the list of available devices that appear on your iPhone's screen.

5. Disconnecting Bluetooth

   C. To disconnect a device or turn off Bluetooth, return to the Bluetooth settings and toggle off the switch next to Bluetooth.

Please note that Bluetooth settings might vary slightly based on the iOS version you're using, but generally, these steps should help you activate Bluetooth on your iPhone.

Follow the easy steps below to connect your hearing aid to your phone.

1. Unlock the iPhone and go to the home screen > Tap on "Settings," ⚙ app > Scroll down and select "Accessibility."

2. Inside the Accessibility menu, scroll down to find and tap on "Hearing Devices."

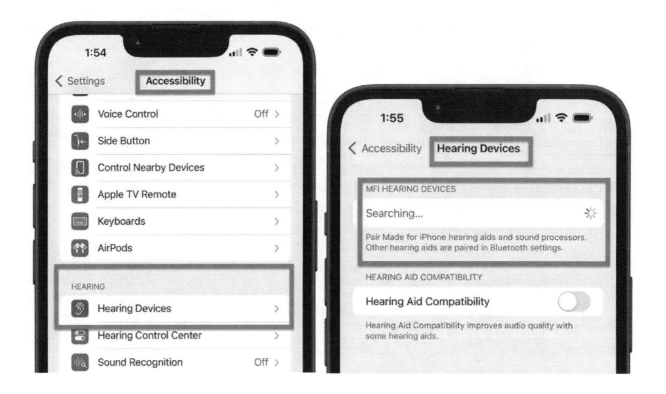

3. Enable Bluetooth

   A. Make sure your hearing aids are in pairing mode and have Bluetooth enabled.

   B. On your iPhone, ensure Bluetooth is activated in the main Settings menu.

4. Pairing Hearing Aids

   A. Your iPhone should detect the hearing aids automatically if they're in pairing mode.

   B. Once they appear on the list of available devices, select your hearing aids to begin the pairing process.

5. Follow On-Screen Instructions

   A. The iPhone will guide you through the pairing process with on-screen instructions.

   B. Follow any prompts that appear to complete the connection setup.

6. Adjust Hearing Aid Settings (if needed)

   A. After successful pairing, there might be additional settings available within the Hearing Devices menu.

B. These settings can vary based on the hearing aid model and might allow further customization or adjustments for the hearing aid's functionality.

7. Test the Connection

A. Verify that the hearing aids are connected by listening to audio or making a test call.

8. Troubleshooting (if necessary)

A. If the devices don't pair successfully, ensure the hearing aids are sufficiently charged, Bluetooth is enabled, and they are within the iPhone's Bluetooth range.

By following these steps, you can seamlessly connect your hearing aids to your iPhone, enhancing your audio experience and allowing for customized sound adjustments tailored to your individual hearing needs.

Visual Alerts

The Visual Alerts feature prompts the iPhone to flash when receiving calls or notifications. This visual cue is immensely helpful for individuals with hearing impairments, ensuring they are alerted to incoming calls or messages, even without relying on auditory cues.

1. Unlock the iPhone and go to the home screen > Tap on "Settings," app > Scroll down and select "Accessibility."

2. Find and Tap on Audio/Visual

A. Inside Accessibility, look for the "Audio/Visual" category.

B. Tap on it to view additional settings related to audio and visual cues.

3. Toggle on LED Flash for Alerts

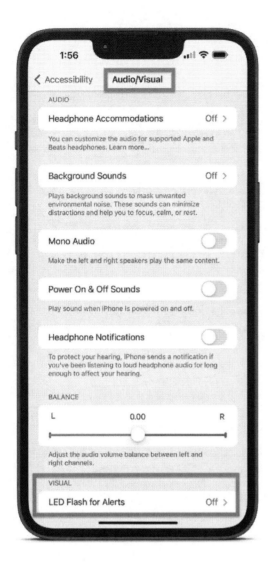

A. Look for the option labeled "LED Flash for Alerts" or similar.

B. Toggle the switch next to it to enable the feature; it will turn green when activated.

C. Once activated, whenever your iPhone receives a call or notification, the LED flash located near the rear camera will flash repeatedly as a visual notification.

By following these steps, you can easily activate Visual Alerts on your iPhone to receive visual cues for incoming calls and notifications, providing an additional layer of accessibility for those with hearing impairments.

Live Listen with AirPods

Live Listen is a feature available on iPhones that allows you to use your device as a remote microphone. It was originally designed to assist individuals with hearing difficulties by using the iPhone's microphone to pick up sounds and stream them directly to their hearing aids.

1. Ensure AirPods are Connected.

    A. Open the AirPods case near your iPhone and ensure they are connected and active.

2. Unlock the iPhone and go to the home screen > Tap on "Settings," 🎯 app > Scroll down and select "Accessibility."

3. Navigate to the Hearing Section

A. Look for the "Hearing" or "Audio/Visual" section within Accessibility.

4. Enable Live Listen

A. Tap on "Audio/Visual" or a similar option.

B. Find the "Live Listen" feature and tap to enable it.

5. Choose AirPods

A. Once Live Listen is activated, a list of available devices will appear.

B. Select your AirPods from the list to pair them with Live Listen.

With Live Listen enabled and AirPods connected, your iPhone becomes a microphone that picks up sound from its surroundings. The sound is then streamed directly to your AirPods, effectively amplifying nearby conversations or sounds. This feature is particularly beneficial in noisy environments or when trying to hear someone speaking from a distance.

By following these steps, you can activate Live Listen with your AirPods, allowing you to utilize your iPhone as a remote microphone for enhanced sound amplification and clarity, especially in challenging listening situations.

Additional Hearing Features in iOS

Video Subtitles

iOS offers support for video subtitles, enhancing accessibility for users with hearing difficulties. These subtitles or closed captions can be enabled on compatible videos, providing a textual representation of dialogue and audio cues.

1. Open Video App

A. Launch the app where you watch videos, like YouTube or Apple's Videos app.

2. Find Subtitle Options

A. Play a video and look for the "Subtitles" or "CC" icon. It's typically represented by "CC" or an icon with speech bubbles.

3. Toggle Subtitles On

A. Tap the "Subtitles" or "CC" icon to enable subtitles.

B. Some apps may have additional settings to customize the appearance or language of subtitles.

Headphone Accommodations

Headphone Accommodations is a feature that enhances audio output when using headphones. It can amplify soft sounds or fine-tune audio frequencies to suit specific hearing profiles, providing a more tailored listening experience.

1. Unlock the iPhone and go to the home screen > Tap on "Settings,"  app > Scroll down and select "Accessibility."

2. Select Audio/Visual

A. Look for "Audio/Visual" or similar options within Accessibility settings.

3. Enable Headphone Accommodations

A. Tap on "Headphone Accommodations."

B. Toggle the switch to enable the feature.

C. Depending on your preference, adjust settings for "Custom Audio Setup" or "Headphone Accommodations" for tailored hearing adjustments.

By utilizing these features, iOS users with hearing difficulties can benefit from subtitles in videos and fine-tuned audio through Headphone Accommodations, fostering a more inclusive and personalized experience while engaging with their devices.

Keeping Track of Your Health

The Health app in iOS offers a robust platform for monitoring and managing personal health metrics. Here's an explanation of the Health Data Tracking and Medical ID Functionality along with a guide on setting up your Medical ID.

Health Data Tracking

The Health app is a versatile tool that allows you to track various health metrics such as:

- steps taken

- sleep patterns

- heart rate

- exercise

- nutrition and more.

Tracking these metrics aids in maintaining an active lifestyle and provides insights into health trends over time.

1. Access the Health App - It's represented by a white icon with a red heart.

2. Browse Health Categories

   A. Explore different categories like "Activity," "Sleep," "Heart," "Nutrition," and more.

   B. Tap on a specific category to view and track related metrics.

3. Add Data Manually (if needed)

   A. Tap "Add Data" to manually input health metrics if your device doesn't track certain data automatically.

Medical ID Functionality

The Medical ID feature within the Health app allows you to store essential medical information such as:

- allergies

- medications

- emergency contacts

- blood type

- existing health conditions and more.

This data is accessible even when the phone is locked, providing crucial information to first responders or medical personnel during emergencies.

1. Open the Health App

   A. Launch the Health app on your iPhone.

2. Tap on Your Profile

   A. Locate and tap the profile icon in the top-right corner.

3. Select Medical ID

   A. Tap on "Medical ID" to set up or edit your medical information.

4. Enter Medical Information

   A. Fill in the necessary fields with your emergency contacts, medical conditions, allergies, medications, and relevant health data.

5. Enable Medical ID on the Lock Screen

   A. Toggle on "Show When Locked" to make this information accessible from the lock screen.

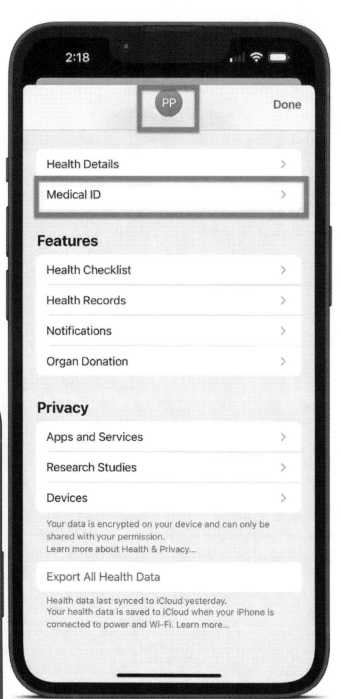

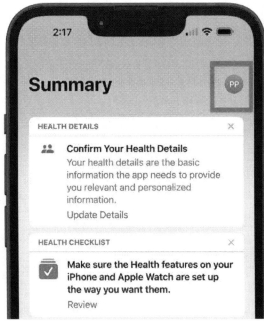

By utilizing these features in the Health app, you can effectively track health metrics and ensure critical medical information is readily available, contributing to better health management and preparedness during emergencies.

Emergency SOS Activation

This feature is designed to offer quick and vital access to critical health information and emergency services during unforeseen situations, ensuring your safety and well-being.

1. Access Unlock the iPhone and go to the home screen > Tap on "Settings,"  app > Scroll down and select " Emergency SOS."

A. Toggle on the "Call with Hold and Release" option.

B. This allows you to call emergency services rapidly, by pressing and holding the side button (on devices with Face ID) along with one of the volume buttons.

C. iPhone will automatically initiate a call to emergency services when Emergency SOS is triggered.

These features are invaluable in critical situations, providing swift access to emergency services and ensuring that vital health information is readily available.

Navigating your iPhone is made seamless with a suite of accessibility features tailored to meet a variety of needs. Whether it's aiding visual impairments, motor skill challenges, or physical limitations, iOS offers a range of tools designed to make your iPhone experience more inclusive and user-friendly. Let's explore more of these features and how they empower users with different abilities.

VoiceOver

VoiceOver serves as a fundamental screen-reading tool specifically designed to assist individuals with visual impairments in navigating their iPhone interface. Its core functionality lies in audibly describing on-screen content and activities. When VoiceOver is enabled, it provides spoken feedback for every touch or gesture on the screen. This auditory feedback assists users in comprehending and interacting with the device's interface. By touching or swiping the screen, users can explore different elements, such as icons, buttons, or text, and VoiceOver will articulate these items, enabling users to navigate through the device and access its functions.

1. Unlock the iPhone and go to the home screen > Tap on "Settings," app > Scroll down and select "Accessibility."

2. Select VoiceOver

   A. Within Accessibility, locate and tap on "VoiceOver."

3. Toggle VoiceOver On

   A. Toggle the switch next to VoiceOver to turn it on. As you do this, your iPhone will begin verbally announcing the items on the screen.

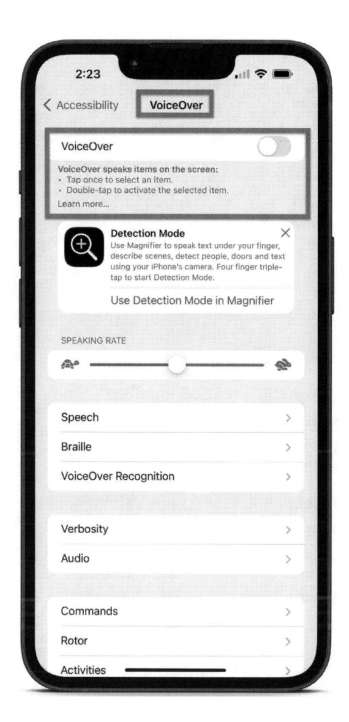

- Adjust Settings (Optional) – Once Voiceover is turned on, you can customize VoiceOver settings by tapping on it. This allows you to adjust speech rate, pitch, and other options to better suit your preferences.

- Once VoiceOver is enabled, you can explore your iPhone's interface by touching and swiping the screen. VoiceOver will provide spoken feedback for each interaction, aiding in navigation and accessibility.

AssistiveTouch

This feature assists users with motor skill impairments by providing alternative controls. AssistiveTouch creates a customizable, floating menu on the screen that allows gesture-based commands. It supports taps, swipes, and multi-finger gestures, easing device navigation.

1. Unlock the iPhone and go to the home screen > Tap on "Settings," 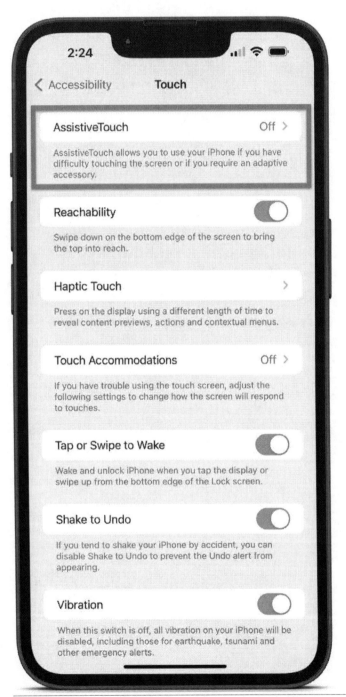 app > Scroll down and select "Accessibility." Under the Accessibility menu, tap on "Touch."

- Locate "AssistiveTouch" and toggle the switch to enable it.

- You can customize the menu by tapping "Customize Top Level Menu." This allows you to add or remove actions or gestures based on your preferences.

Once enabled, a small circle will appear on your screen, serving as the AssistiveTouch menu. You can use this menu to perform various gestures and actions, providing an alternative way to control your iPhone.

Switch Control

Geared toward individuals with physical impairments, Switch Control allows device operation via external switches, joysticks, or buttons. Customizable scanning modes enable navigation and selection via sequential or personalized scanning actions, empowering users to operate their devices according to their capabilities.

1. Unlock the iPhone and go to the home screen > Tap on "Settings," app > Scroll down and select "Accessibility." Under the Accessibility menu, tap on "Switch Control."

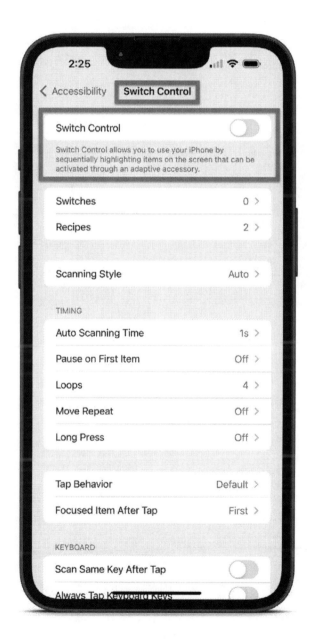

- Toggle the switch to enable "Switch Control."

- Configure Switches (if needed) - You can connect external switches or devices by tapping "Switches." Follow the on-screen instructions to set up and configure your switches for device control.

Once activated, Switch Control allows for navigation and interaction with your iPhone using the connected external switches or devices, enhancing accessibility for individuals with physical impairments

Translation Apps

Translation apps open doors to a world without language barriers. From everyday conversations to exploring new cultures, these apps decode languages on the go, making communication a breeze.

Apple's Translate

This app comes pre-installed with iOS 15 or later, so there's no need for a separate download. It's capable of translating text and speech in 12 languages and conversations in 11 languages. Sporting an easy-to-use interface, it functions offline or on your device, ensuring your privacy. However, it doesn't support camera translation, image translation, handwriting, or textbook translation.

Google Translate

This app stands as one of the most widely used and versatile translation tools. It can handle text, speech, images, and chat across a whopping 133 languages. It offers offline translation, snapshot translation, image translation, interactive translation, handwriting, and sentence book features. However, please be mindful that many of the features demand an internet connection and translation might not be entirely accurate or native across all languages.

SayHi Translation

This app brings a fun and welcoming vibe to translations. It covers 100 languages and dialects, offering a "Universal Translator" feature for seamless chats between individuals speaking different languages. Additionally, it allows customization of voices and tones for your translations. However, it doesn't support text translation, offline translation, camera translation, image translation, handwriting, or textbook translation.

iOS 17 Accessibility Features

With the latest operating system update, the iOS 17 comes with a range of new accessibility futures and improvements that we can't ignore. The iOS 17 update brings numerous accessibility enhancements to iPhones, aimed at making them more user-friendly for all. Siri's speech speed can now be adjusted, allowing users to customize its pace. A new feature, Live Speech, types as you speak, benefiting those with speech difficulties. Personal Voice creates a voice clone, ensuring your iPhone sounds like you. Assistive Access simplifies the interface for users with cognitive challenges. Voice Control offers a tutorial for easy adoption, guiding users through voice-command operation. The Magnifier Detection Mode aids in text recognition, reading text aloud, and correcting it using Voice Control. GIFs in Messages now auto-pause after playing. Users can also customize Spoken Content voices and use Switch Control as a virtual game controller, enhancing accessibility across various functions.

Staying Active With the Fitness App

The Fitness app on the iPhone isn't just a basic activity tracker—it's a comprehensive tool designed to support and motivate your fitness journey. This app goes beyond counting steps; it monitors daily activity, including steps, distance, and elevation, offering detailed insights to help set goals and track progress. But it doesn't stop there—it also offers guided workouts for various fitness levels and preferences, both at home and through the Apple Fitness+ subscription service. Fitness+ offers a vast library of interactive workout videos led by professional trainers, covering diverse exercise types like cycling, yoga, and strength training. These sessions are interactive, displaying real-time metrics on-screen and syncing seamlessly with your Apple Watch for a complete fitness experience.

Steps to Access and Utilize the Fitness App

1. Locate and tap the "Fitness" app on your iPhone's home screen – It typically showcases your daily activity summary and offers tabs for various features like workouts and health data.

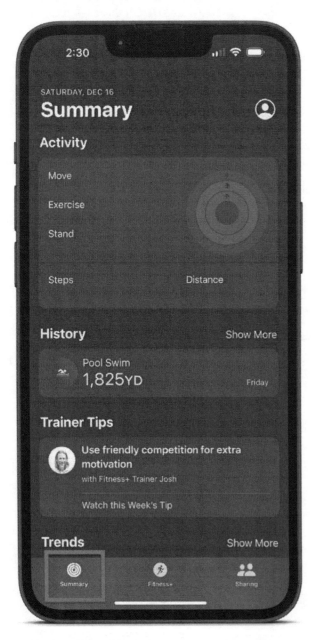
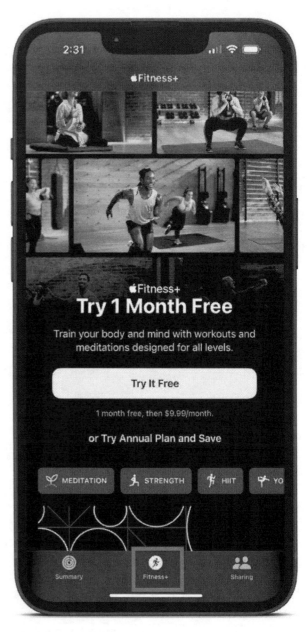

2. Activity Tracking

    A. Explore your daily activity stats displayed within the app.

    B. These include steps taken, distance covered, and flights of stairs climbed, offering insights into your movement patterns and overall activity level.

3. Setting Goals

    A. Within the Fitness app, set personalized activity goals based on your preferences and fitness ambitions.

    B. This feature allows you to track and measure progress over time, keeping you motivated to maintain an active lifestyle.

4. Guided Workouts

    A. Navigate to the "Workouts" section in the app to access a collection of guided workouts tailored to different fitness levels and preferences.

    B. Choose from various workout types and durations to match your interests and schedule.

5. Apple Fitness+

    A. To access the extensive library of interactive workouts available through Fitness+, open the Fitness app and explore the Fitness+ tab.

    B. Subscribe to Fitness+ to unlock an array of professionally led workout videos, complete with real-time metrics and diverse exercise categories.

6. Personalization

    A. Customize your workout routines and preferences within Fitness+ to align with your fitness goals and interests.

    B. Tailor your experience by selecting workout types, durations, and instructors that suit your needs.

Remember, the Fitness app is an all-encompassing tool that not only tracks your activity but also offers guidance and motivation through various workout options. Explore its features to enjoy a personalized fitness journey that suits your lifestyle and preferences.

Optimizing your iPhone for accessibility and usability significantly enhances its functionality especially if you're looking for a more user-friendly interface. By adjusting settings such as:

- text size and icon visibility

- accessibility shortcuts for quick access

- enabling features like VoiceOver and the Magnifier tool.

You can adapt the device to your needs and further simplify navigation and usage with functions like AssistiveTouch and Siri.

Additionally, safety features like Emergency SOS and organizational methods such as arranging the home screen and streamlining apps contribute to a more seamless user experience. Setting up emergency contacts and storing tech support information adds a layer of support in times of need. With these enhancements, the iPhone becomes an inclusive, supportive, and efficient tool tailored to your individual preferences and requirements, paving the way for an enriched user experience.

Now that you're equipped with personalized settings, it's time to explore the device's incredible camera technology and capture life's memorable moments.

CHAPTER 9

Capturing and Cherishing Moments: Guide to iPhone Photography and Videography

When words become unclear, I shall focus with photographs.
When images become inadequate, I shall be content with silence.
—Ansel Adams

Everything thus far has been exciting; however, the real fun is about to start now. Yes, I'm talking about how you can successfully capture those priceless moments on camera. No more need for dragging around an additional camera or video recorder, because your iPhone can do it all. Plus, there's no need to have a film developed or get a professional to give you your photos. No, you can simply snap and send that moment to everyone you wish to share it with.

In this chapter, we will cover it all, from basic camera functions, to how to operate the camera, send and store pictures, and everything in between.

Snap, Store, and Share: Mastering the iPhone Camera

Capturing life's moments with your iPhone's camera is an enriching experience, allowing you to preserve cherished memories in vivid detail. The iPhone's camera is a versatile tool capable of capturing everything from everyday adventures to significant milestones. For instance, imagine the sheer delight of capturing your granddaughter's first ballet performance in a high-quality video and effortlessly sharing it with family members residing miles away.

To make the most of your iPhone camera start with basic techniques like focusing by:

1. tapping on the screen

2. adjusting exposure levels by sliding your finger up or down

3. using gridlines for better composition.

Experiment with different angles, perspectives, and lighting conditions to discover what works best for your photos or videos.

- The iPhone offers an array of modes catering to diverse shooting scenarios.

- The Photo mode captures still images, while the Video mode records motion.

- SlowMo slows down the action for dramatic effect.

- Time-lapse creates accelerated videos

- and Panorama captures wide-angle scenes.

Each mode has its unique attributes and is accessible from the camera interface, allowing you to choose the right mode for each moment.

Moreover, statistics from Statista in 2020 highlight that 89% of seniors use their smartphones primarily for taking photos, underlining its popularity among this age group. This indicates that many seniors find joy and value in using their smartphones, especially the camera, to document and share their experiences. Embracing these simple yet powerful tips and exploring the diverse modes of iPhone photography can elevate your photography and videography skills, enabling you to capture life's beautiful moments effortlessly.

The iPhone camera offers an array of versatile modes tailored for various photography and videography needs.

Understanding these modes empowers you to capture diverse moments effectively.

1. **Photo Mode**: Ideal for regular pictures, offering numerous settings for adjustments.

2. **Portrait Mode**: Creates a blurred background effect (bokeh) for portrait shots, emphasizing the subject.

3. **Pano (Panoramic) Mode**: Captures wide landscape images by stitching multiple photos together horizontally.

4. **Video Mode**: Records standard motion videos, suitable for capturing events or activities.

5. **Action Mode**: Optimized for capturing fast-moving subjects with a higher shutter speed.

6. **Slo-Mo (Slow Motion) Mode**: Records videos at a high frame rate, playing back in slow motion for dramatic effect.

7. **Time-Lapse Mode**: Captures a series of images at set intervals, creating a fast-motion video sequence.

8. **Cinematic Mode (Newer Models)**: Simulates a depth-of-field effect in videos, blurring the background for a cinematic look.

Changing camera modes on an iPhone is incredibly user-friendly. When you open the Camera app, you can effortlessly switch between different modes.

1. Access Camera Modes

   A. Open the Camera app on your iPhone.

   B. Swipe left or right on the camera screen to switch between different modes.

   C. Alternatively, tap the icons at the bottom of the screen to navigate directly to specific modes like Photo, Video, Slow-Mo, Time-Lapse, and more.

Regarding zoom functionality, iPhones offer two distinct types of zoom:

1. Optical Zoom

   This uses the physical lenses within the camera system to magnify without compromising image quality. It's typically available on dual or triple-lens camera setups, such as on newer iPhone models like the iPhone 12 Pro Max or iPhone 13 Pro Max.

2. Digital Zoom

   This method enlarges the image by cropping and digitally magnifying the pixels using software. However, it may lead to a loss of image quality as it enlarges the picture.

Experimenting with these modes, zoom capabilities, and other settings allows you to become more familiar with your iPhone's camera features. It's a fantastic way to explore the camera's potential and find innovative ways to capture stunning moments and memories. So don't hesitate to explore and unleash your creativity!

Organizing Your Memories: Managing Your Photos and Videos

Organizing your photos and videos into albums within the Photos app on your iPhone can significantly streamline the way you navigate and share your memories. Here's how you can create albums and group similar content together.

Creating an Album

1. Unlock the iPhone and go to the home screen > locate and Tap on the "Photos" App icon to open it.

2. **Navigate to Albums** - At the bottom of the screen, locate and tap on the "Albums" tab. This section holds all your existing albums and is where you'll create a new one.

3. Create a New Album

   A. Look for the "+" (Add) icon, typically situated in the top-left or bottom-right corner of the Albums screen.

   B. Tap the "+" icon to add a new album to your collection.

   C. From the options that appear, select "New Album."

4. Name Your Album

   A. Upon selecting "New Album," a dialog box will prompt you to give your album a name.

   B. Enter a descriptive and easily recognizable name for your new album, such as "Family Vacations" or "Garden Pictures."

   C. Once you've named the album, tap "Save" or "Done" to create it.

Creating specific albums with descriptive names allows you to efficiently categorize and locate your photos and videos later on. This organization simplifies the process of finding and sharing specific moments or themes captured in your iPhone's photo library.

Adding Photos or Videos to an Album

1. Navigate to the Album

   A. Open the "Photos" app on your iPhone.

   B. Tap on the "Albums" tab at the bottom of the screen.

   C. Locate and select the specific album to which you wish to add new content.

2. Select Photos or Videos

   A. Inside the chosen album, tap on the "Select" option positioned at the top-right corner of the screen.

   B. Browse through your photo library and tap on the individual photos or videos you want to add to the album.

   C. Selected items usually show a checkmark or are highlighted.

3. Add to Album

   A. After selecting the desired photos or videos, look for the "Add" or "Done" button at the bottom or top-right corner of the screen (the wording might differ based on your iOS version).

   B. Tap "Add" or "Done" to include the selected items in the specific album.

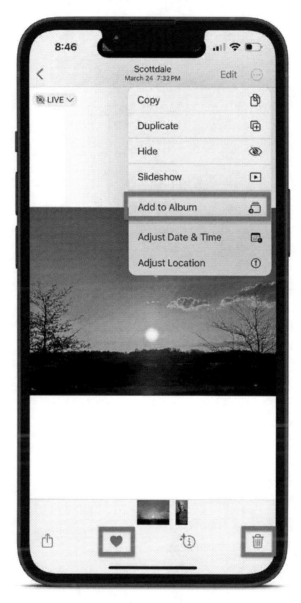

By following these steps, you can easily organize and group your photos or videos within designated albums, making it simpler to manage and share your cherished moments with ease.

Organizing or Editing Albums

Rearrange Photo Order

1. View All Items

    A. Open the specific album you want to organize.

    B. Tap on "See All" to display all the photos or videos within the album.

2. Reorder Photos

    A. Tap "Select" located in the top-right corner.

    B. Drag the individual photos or videos to rearrange their order within the album.

    C. Once you've arranged them as desired, tap "Done" or a similar option to save the changes.

Editing or Deleting Albums

1. Access Album Settings

    A. Go to the "Albums" tab in the Photos app.

    B. Tap "Edit" typically found in the top-right corner of the screen.

    C. To edit an album's details, such as its name, tap on the album you wish to modify.

Deleting Unwanted Photos

Single Photo Deletion

1. Access Photos App on your iPhone.

2. Select and Delete

    A. Navigate to the photo or video you want to delete.

    B. Tap on the item to open it.

    C. Tap the trash can icon (usually located at the bottom right or top left).

    D. Confirm the deletion by selecting "Delete Photo" or "Delete Video."

Bulk Deletion

1. Access Recently Deleted Album

   A. Open the "Photos" app and go to the "Albums" tab.

   B. Scroll down and select "Recently Deleted."

2. Select Items to Permanently Delete

   A. Tap "Select" located at the top right corner.

   B. Choose the photos or videos you want to permanently delete by tapping on each item.

3. Delete Permanently

   A. Tap "Delete" or the trash can icon. Confirm the action to permanently remove the selected items from your device.

Tip: Deleted photos and videos are moved to the "Recently Deleted" album where they remain for 30 days before being permanently deleted from your device. Within this 30-day window, you can recover mistakenly deleted items from this album. After 30 days, they are automatically removed permanently.

Creating specific albums like "Family Vacations" or "Garden Pictures" serves as an efficient method to categorize and organize related content, facilitating easier access and sharing. This streamlined approach simplifies the retrieval of specific photos or videos, ensuring that you can easily relive your cherished memories whenever desired.

Backing Up Your Memories

Regularly backing up your photos and videos to iCloud safeguards them against accidental loss or damage to your iPhone. It's a reliable way to preserve cherished memories even if something happens to your device.

Using iCloud Backup

1. Open the "Settings" app on your iPhone > **Access iCloud Settings**

   A. Tap your name at the top of the screen to access your Apple ID settings.

   B. Select "iCloud" from the options.

2. **Enable iCloud Backup**

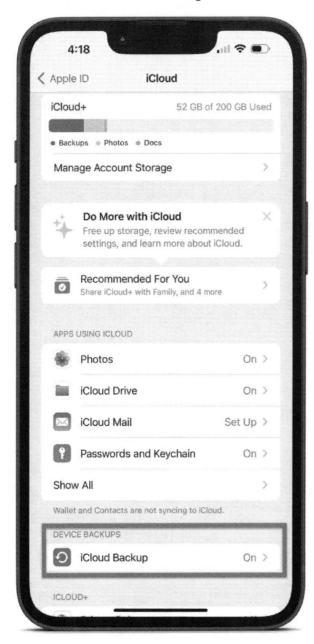

Enable iCloud Backup

A. Scroll down and tap "iCloud Backup."

B. Toggle on "iCloud Backup" if it's not already enabled.

C. Ensure your iPhone is connected to a Wi-Fi network for automatic backups.

Automatic Backup

A. Once enabled, iCloud Backup will automatically back up your photos, videos, and other data when your device is connected to Wi-Fi.

This ensures your memories are securely stored in the cloud, minimizing the risk of data loss.

Alternative Backup Options

1. **Google Photos**

   • Offers free storage for high-quality photos and videos.

   • Syncs seamlessly across iOS and Android devices, providing convenient access and easy sharing features.

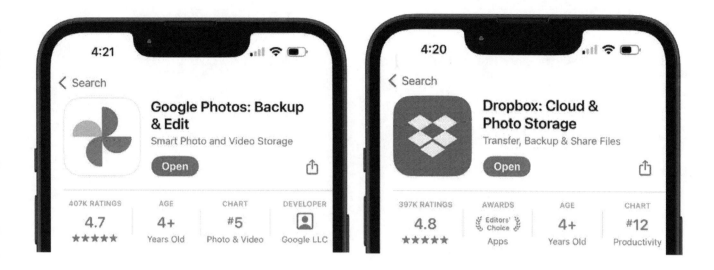

2. **Dropbox**

   - Provides automatic photo backup and file syncing across multiple devices.

   - Offers a user-friendly interface and allows organizing photos into folders and albums for better management.

3. **Amazon Photos**

   - Amazon Prime members receive free unlimited storage for photos.

   - Ensures secure storage and integrates well with various devices for easy access.

4. **Microsoft OneDrive**

- Offers storage space and automatic backup for photos and videos.

- Syncs seamlessly across devices and integrates with Microsoft Office applications.

5. **External Hard Drives**

- Physical storage devices provide tangible backup solutions.

- Connect these drives to your computer and use software to transfer and manage your media files.

These alternative options vary in storage capacity and features, providing secure backup solutions beyond iCloud's storage limitations. Choosing the right option depends on your storage needs and preferences for accessing and managing your backed-up photos and videos.

Sharing Your Moments: Sending Photos and Videos to Loved Ones

Connecting through shared memories enhances the joy of special moments. In this section, we'll unravel the art of sharing your cherished photos and videos with loved ones, exploring the intricacies of messaging, social media platforms, and collaborative album creation. Learn how to effortlessly share your captured stories, foster shared experiences, and weave a tapestry of memories that binds hearts together. As we embark on this journey of connectivity, we'll also delve into the maintenance essentials to keep your device primed for capturing new adventures.

Sharing Through Messages or Mail

When sharing media through Messages on your iPhone, the process is streamlined for quick and direct communication.

1. Selecting Media

    A. Open the Photos app and navigate to the specific photo or video you want to share. Tap on it to select it for sharing.

2. Accessing Share Options

   A. Look for the share button, which typically resembles a square with an upward-pointing arrow. Tap on this icon to initiate the sharing process.

3. Choosing Messages

   A. Within the list of available sharing options, locate and select the Messages app. This action directs the chosen media to a new message.

4. Selecting Contacts

   A. Once in the Messages app, choose the contact or multiple contacts you wish to send the media to. You can type the contact's name or select from your contacts list.

5. Optional Message Addition

   A. If you want to include a personalized message along with the media, tap on the text field within the message window and type your message.

6. Sending the Message

   A. After composing your message (if desired), tap the "Send" button to deliver the media and any accompanying message to the selected contact(s).

This straightforward method enables you to swiftly share photos or videos with friends, family, or colleagues directly through the Messages app, fostering seamless communication through visual content.

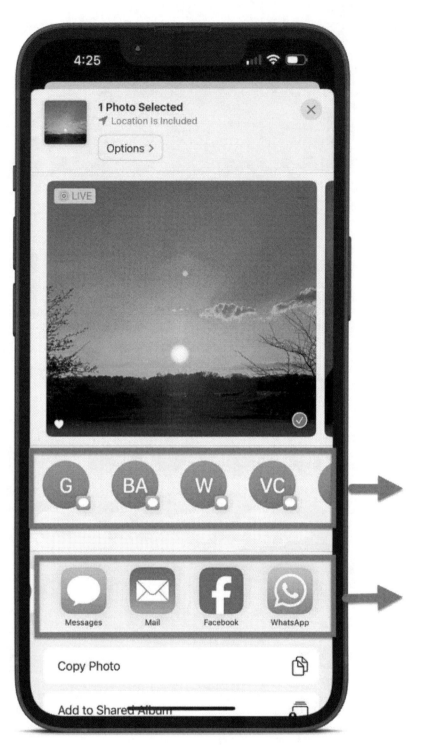

Share your photos or videos with your contacts through the messages app.

Share your photos or videos on social media using installed apps.

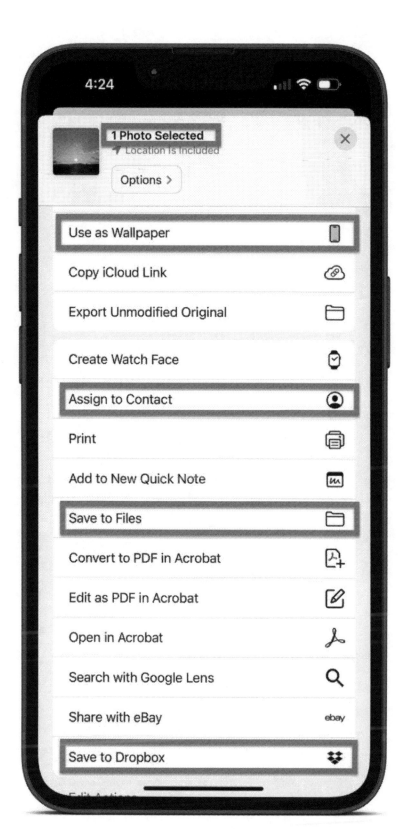

Use a photo in any of the below ways:

- Use as wallpaper

- Assign to a contact

- Save to files

- Save to Dropbox

- Create a iWatch Face

Sharing on Social Media

Sharing your captured moments on social media platforms like Facebook or Instagram is a common way to engage with your network and showcase your experiences. Here's how you can effectively share your photos or videos on these platforms.

1. Selecting Media

    A. Open the Photos app and navigate to the photo or video you want to share.

2. Accessing Share Options

    A. Look for the share button (usually represented by a square with an upward-pointing arrow) and tap on it.

3. Choosing Social Media Apps

    A. From the available sharing options, locate and select the desired social media app, such as Facebook or Instagram.

4. Adding Details

    A. Once the selected app opens, you can include essential details like captions, tags, locations, or other necessary information related to the photo or video you're sharing.

5. Posting Content

    A. After adding the required information, tap the "Share" or "Post" button to upload the content to your chosen social media platform.

Facebook

1. Open the Facebook app and access your profile or news feed.

2. Tap the "Photo" option, and select the photo/video you want to share.

3. Add descriptions, tags, locations, or any necessary information, then tap "Post" to share it on your feed or profile.

Instagram

1. Open Instagram and tap the "+" icon to create a new post.

2. Choose a photo or video from your library.

3. Apply filters, effects, or adjustments if desired.

4. Include a caption and any relevant hashtags or location tags.

5. Tap "Share" to post it on your Instagram profile or story.

Important reminder: It's crucial to regularly review and adjust your privacy settings in social media apps. This allows you to control who can view and interact with your shared content, ensuring your privacy and security online.

Creating a Shared Album

Creating a shared album through your iPhone's Photos app is an excellent way to collectively curate memories and experiences with others. Here's a detailed guide on how to create and manage shared albums.

1. Accessing the Photos App

   A. Open the Photos app on your iPhone to initiate the process.

2. Selecting Content

   A. Tap "Select" and choose the specific photos or videos you want to include in the shared album.

3. Initiating Sharing

   A. Look for the share button, often depicted as a square icon with an upward arrow, and tap it.

4. Creating the Album

   A. From the available options, select "Add to Shared Album" to begin creating a shared album.

5. Naming the Album

   A. Give the album a descriptive name that represents its content or theme, such as "Family Holiday" or any title that reflects the shared experience.

6. Adding Participants

   A. Tap "Next" to add email addresses or contacts of the individuals you wish to invite to the shared album. You can also generate a public link for broader access.

7. Sending Invitations

   A. Confirm and tap "Create" to finalize the shared album and dispatch invitations. Invited participants will receive notifications, allowing them to view and contribute to the album.

For example, in a gardening group, members can actively contribute images of plants, garden layouts, or successful harvests to a shared album named "Gardening Adventures." This collaborative platform enables everyone involved to contribute their perspectives and relish collective memories.

Having explored the intricacies of iPhone photography, let's now delve into strategies to optimize and preserve your device's performance, ensuring it's consistently ready for your next memorable adventure.

CHAPTER 10

Keeping Your iPhone in Top Shape

If there's another iPhone that's better, that's sad for my old iPhone. But it means we get to use a better one.
— Roger Ver

Navigating the intricacies of an iPhone is like embarking on a journey through a digital landscape rich with opportunities. However, just as with any adventure, ensuring a smooth and enjoyable experience requires careful preparation and maintenance. In this chapter, we delve into the art of keeping your iPhone in top shape. From optimizing performance to troubleshooting common issues, we'll explore the various strategies and techniques that empower you to wield your device with confidence and efficiency. Join me on this last adventure for now, and uncover the secrets to maintaining a seamless iPhone experience, unlocking the full potential of this remarkable technological marvel.

Reviving a Frozen iPhone

When an iPhone freezes or becomes unresponsive, it can disrupt your user experience. But fear not, as there's a troubleshooting method that often works like a charm — the hard reset. This technique, while uncommon on modern phones, can sometimes save the day when software-related issues strike.

Here's a step-by-step guide to performing a hard reset, a simple yet potent remedy for an unresponsive iPhone.

Hard Reset Process (Restarting a Frozen iPhone)

1. Press and Hold

   A. Simultaneously press and hold the side button (also known as the sleep/wake button) and the volume down button.

2. Continue Holding

   A. Even if the power-off slider appears on the screen, keep holding both buttons steadfastly.

3. Slide to Power Off

   A. Should the power-off slider make an appearance, disregard it and persist in holding the side and volume down buttons until the screen goes completely black.

   B. This might take around 10 seconds or longer.

4. Restart

   A. Once the device powers off completely, release the buttons.

   B. Then, press and hold the side button again until the iconic Apple logo graces your screen.

   C. Typically, this takes just a few seconds.

It's essential to note that a hard reset doesn't erase any data on your iPhone; rather, it acts as a forceful reboot when the device encounters a freeze. If the problem persists post-reset or if your iPhone frequently experiences freezing episodes, seeking additional support from Apple or a certified technician might be wise.

When your iPhone encounters persistent issues or glitches, a force restart might be the trick to get things back on track. This method, known as an alternative restart or force restart, can serve as another solution if standard troubleshooting falls short.

Force Restart (Alternative Restart Method)

Here's how to execute a force restart.

1. Quick Button Press

    A. Swiftly press and release the volume up button, followed by the volume down button in quick succession.

2. Hold Side Button

    A. After the quick button presses, hold down the side button (also referred to as the sleep/wake button) until the Apple logo makes its appearance on the screen.

In cases where problems persist despite restarting your device, updating to the latest iOS version could be the key. Apple regularly rolls out updates containing bug fixes and enhancements that specifically target common issues. Updating your device's software might just provide the solution you need.

Updating iOS

Updating your iPhone's iOS can be a pivotal step in resolving persistent issues or glitches. Here's a breakdown of how to update your iOS.

1. Open the Settings ⚙ app on your iPhone.

2. Scroll down and tap on "General."

3. Select Software Update

    A. Look for "Software Update" and tap on it.

4. Download and Install

    A. If an update is available, tap "Download and Install" to commence the update process.

These steps predominantly focus on addressing software-related problems. However, if your iPhone persists in experiencing issues or encounters hardware-related challenges, seeking guidance from Apple Support or a certified technician might be necessary for comprehensive assistance and support.

Freeing Up Storage

Managing storage and adjusting background app settings can significantly improve your iPhone's performance and battery life. Here's how to effectively free up storage space.

Checking Storage Usage

1. Open the Settings app on your iPhone.

2. Scroll down and tap on "General."

3. Select iPhone Storage

    A. Tap on "iPhone Storage" to view the storage breakdown.

Reviewing and Removing Items

1. Identify Large Files

    A. Review the listed apps and files to identify large storage consumers.

2. Delete Unnecessary Items

    A. Remove unnecessary apps, large files, or old photos/videos that occupy significant space.

App Removal Process

1. Select App for Removal

    A. Tap on an app listed under storage settings.

2. Delete App

    A. Choose "Delete App" to uninstall it from your device.

Clearing Cache

1. Identify Apps with Cache

    A. Certain apps accumulate cache data.

2. Uninstall and Reinstall

A. For apps with cache buildup (e.g., browsers), uninstalling and reinstalling them can help clear the cache and free up space.

By periodically managing storage and removing unnecessary apps or files, you can optimize your iPhone's storage capacity and potentially enhance its overall performance.

Background App Refresh

Managing the Background App Refresh settings can significantly impact your iPhone's battery life and overall performance.

1. Open the Settings ⚙ app on your iPhone.

2. Scroll down and tap on "General."

3. Background App Refresh

A. Tap on "Background App Refresh."

Managing App Refresh Settings

1. Disable Specific Apps

A. Toggle off the option for apps that don't require constant updates or aren't frequently used.

2. Customize Refresh Preferences

A. Adjust settings for each app, enabling only essential apps to refresh in the background.

Background App Refresh permits apps to update content in the background, ensuring they display the latest information upon opening. However, this continuous updating consumes battery power by regularly fetching data even when apps aren't actively in use.

By disabling Background App Refresh for non-essential apps, you can conserve battery life. Restricting background activities of less frequently used apps minimizes unnecessary battery consumption, leading to prolonged battery performance.

Managing background app refresh settings not only preserves battery life but also improves the overall performance of your iPhone, particularly for older devices or those experiencing sluggishness.

Addressing Battery Drain Issues

Optimizing battery usage on your iPhone is essential, especially for individuals heavily reliant on their devices. Here are additional methods to address battery drain issues.

Optimizing Screen Brightness

1. Auto-Brightness Setting

   A. Enable Auto-Brightness

      a) Access Settings > Display & Brightness.

      b) Turn on Auto-Brightness, allowing the iPhone to adjust screen brightness based on ambient light conditions.

   B. This feature conserves battery power by automatically reducing screen brightness in well-lit environments.

2. Manual Brightness Adjustment

   A. Manual Brightness Control

   B. If Auto-Brightness isn't preferred, manually adjust the brightness slider in Settings > Display & Brightness.

   C. Lowering the screen brightness manually, particularly in low-light settings, can significantly extend battery life.

Managing Location Services

1. Access Location Services Settings: Navigate to Settings > Privacy > Location Services.

2. Disable Unnecessary Access

A. Turn off location services for apps that don't require constant access to your device's location.

B. Limiting apps' access to location data can notably improve battery performance by reducing background location-related activities.

By optimizing screen brightness settings and managing location services, you can effectively address battery drain issues on your iPhone, ensuring prolonged battery life for your device.

App Usage and Background Activity

Taking care of your iPhone's battery life is crucial for ensuring it lasts throughout the day. Let me delve deeper into each of these points.

1. Tap on the "Settings" app on your iPhone's home screen.

2. Go to Battery Settings

    A. Scroll down and select "Battery."

3. Review Battery Usage

    A. In the Battery settings, you'll find the "Battery Usage by App" section. Tap on it to see which apps are consuming the most power.

Closing Background Apps

1. Access App Switcher

    A. Swipe up from the bottom of the screen and hold briefly. This action will bring up the app switcher, displaying all the apps currently running.

2. Close Background Apps

    A. Swipe up on the app cards that are running in the background but aren't actively being used. This action will close those apps and stop their background processes.

Update Apps and iOS

Keep your apps updated to their latest versions. Developers often release updates that optimize battery usage, fix bugs, and enhance performance.

1. Open the "Settings"  app on your iPhone. Scroll down and select "General."

2. Tap on "Software Update." If a new iOS version is available, follow the on-screen instructions to download and install it.

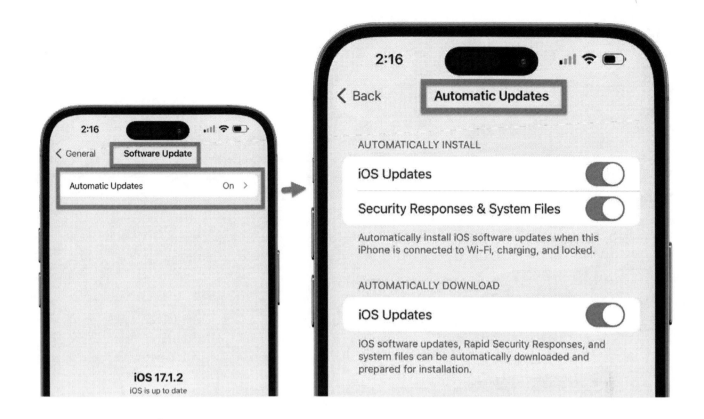

Following these step-by-step instructions can help you efficiently manage your iPhone's battery life and ensure that it remains reliable throughout the day.

Implementing these steps not only improves battery life but also contributes to a smoother and more efficient overall experience with your iPhone.

Enabling Low Power Mode

When Low Power Mode is activated, some visual effects like motion effects and animated wallpapers may be reduced or turned off to save battery. Background app refresh, mail fetch, and some visual effects are limited to help conserve battery life. The screen brightness might dim, and the auto-lock setting may be adjusted to conserve power.

1. Tap on the "Settings" ![icon] app from your iPhone's home screen.

2. Scroll down and select "Battery."

3. Activate Low Power Mode

    A. Toggle on the "Low Power Mode" option. This action can be done by tapping the switch next to "Low Power Mode." The switch turns green when activated.

Your iPhone prompts you to activate Low Power Mode when the battery reaches 20% and 10% remaining charge. You can also manually enable it at any battery percentage to conserve power.

Low Power Mode conserves battery life by reducing the background activity and some visual effects, ensuring your iPhone lasts longer on a single charge.

While in Low Power Mode, core functionality like calls, texts, and other essential features still work; however, some non-essential background tasks may be delayed or paused.

Activating Low Power Mode can be particularly helpful when you're low on battery and need to extend your iPhone's usage until you can recharge it. It's a useful feature to have for conserving power in critical situations.

Further Battery-Saving Tips

Adjusting Battery Life Settings

1. **Shorten Auto-Lock Time**

   A. Open "Settings" 🔧 > "Display & Brightness" > "Auto-Lock."

   B. Choose a shorter duration for the auto-lock feature, such as 30 seconds or 1 minute, to conserve power when your iPhone is inactive.

2. **Reduce Screen Timeout**

   A. Go to "Settings" 🔧 > "Display & Brightness."

   B. Adjust the "Timeout" or "Screen Off" duration to minimize how long the screen stays on when not in use.

Turning Off Non-Essential Features

1. **Disable Dynamic Wallpapers**

   A. Navigate to "Settings" 🔧 > "Wallpaper."

   B. Choose a static wallpaper instead of dynamic ones to reduce battery usage.

2. **Turn Off Motion Effects**

   A. Access "Settings" 🔧 > "Accessibility" > "Motion."

B. Disable motion effects like Parallax, which can consume battery power.

Avoiding Intensive Apps

Games and video streaming apps can drain the battery quickly. Limit their usage, especially when your battery is low or during critical times.

Using the Right Charger & Cable

Always use certified chargers and cables to avoid potential damage to the battery or inconsistent charging.

Disabling Push Notifications

1. Open "Settings" > "Notifications."

   Disable unnecessary notifications or limit the number of apps sending them to conserve battery life.

Optimizing Background App Refresh

1. Access "Settings" > "General" > "Background App Refresh."

   Disable this feature for apps that don't require real-time updates or whose background activity isn't essential.

Managing Mail Fetch Settings

1. Go to "Settings" > "Mail" > "Accounts" > "Fetch New Data."

   Set email accounts to fetch manually or at longer intervals to reduce frequent data updates.

Keeping Your iPhone Cool

High temperatures can degrade battery life. Keep your iPhone away from direct sunlight or extremely hot environments to maintain battery health.

Implementing these battery-saving tips can significantly extend your iPhone's battery life, ensuring it remains efficient during crucial moments and essential tasks. Conserving battery power enhances the overall performance and reliability of your device, especially when you need it the most.

Maintaining proper charging practices is vital for preserving iPhone battery health. Here's a detailed guide:

Understanding Battery Charge Cycles

A charge cycle completes when you've used the entirety of your battery's capacity, from 100% to near 0%. Typically, iPhones endure around 500 complete charge cycles before experiencing significant battery capacity reduction.

Avoid Zero Battery

Maintaining your iPhone's battery within the range of 20-80% is ideal for longevity. Avoid frequent complete discharges to 0% for better battery health.

Avoid Overnight Charging

iPhones employ optimized charging to delay reaching 100% until needed, preserving long-term battery health. Leaving it plugged in overnight doesn't keep it continuously charging to 100%.

Avoid Simultaneous Charging and Usage

Charging your iPhone while running power-intensive apps can generate excess heat, impacting battery health. It's advisable to avoid this scenario when possible.

Use Official Apple Chargers

Using certified Apple chargers and cables ensures compatibility and reduces potential damage to the battery. Non-certified accessories might not deliver consistent power.

Troubleshooting Battery Drain

Identifying and resolving issues that cause excessive battery drain helps preserve your iPhone's battery health. By addressing these problems, you can extend the overall lifespan of your battery and maintain its optimal performance over time.

Battery drain caused by inefficient apps or background processes can affect your device's overall performance. By troubleshooting and managing these issues, you ensure that your iPhone operates smoothly and efficiently, without unnecessary lags or disruptions.

Unexpected battery drain can disrupt your daily usage by necessitating frequent recharges or causing your device to shut down unexpectedly. Troubleshooting helps maintain a consistent user experience by preventing such disruptions and ensuring your device remains reliable throughout the day.

1. Check Battery Usage

   Navigate to Settings > Battery to access insights into which apps consume the most power. This feature is pivotal for efficient management of app usage that affects your battery life.

2. Identify Battery Drain Culprits

   Monitoring battery usage helps uncover apps, including popular ones, causing unexpected drains due to inefficiencies in their coding or features.

3. Home Screen Widget Management

   Widgets, especially those frequently refreshing data, can contribute to battery drain. Managing and reducing their presence on the home screen can significantly conserve battery life.

4. Managing Background Activity

   Disable Background Refresh for apps draining significant battery despite rare use. Consider uninstalling non-essential apps as an alternative solution to curb battery drain caused by background processes.

Resolving App Malfunctions

App Not Responding

1. Force Close App

   When an app freezes or behaves abnormally, take action by double-clicking the home button (for older models) or swiping up from the bottom (for newer models) to access the app switcher. From there, locate the problematic app and swipe it up to close it forcefully.

Deleting and Reinstalling Apps

1. Delete App

    If issues persist, remove the problematic app by pressing and holding its icon until a menu appears. Choose "Delete App" to remove it.

2. Reinstall from App Store

    Head to the App Store to reinstall the app. This step often resolves glitches or issues that persist after deletion.

Updating Apps

Ensure apps are up to date as developers frequently release updates to address bugs and enhance performance. Open the App Store, tap your profile icon, and check for pending updates. Proceed to update the apps needing attention.

Following these troubleshooting steps effectively manages battery drain caused by apps, contributing to a smoother iPhone experience. Resolving app-related issues through force closing, deleting, reinstalling, and updating apps further promotes stable and efficient device usage.

When All Else Fails: Factory Resetting Your iPhone

A factory reset is a powerful solution, reserved for situations when all other fixes have hit a dead end. It's like hitting the refresh button, restoring your iPhone to its brand-new, out-of-the-box state. While it's a rare and drastic measure, it holds the key to solving complex issues that might stump other troubleshooting methods.

But fear not! Before diving into a factory reset, take charge and safeguard your precious data. Back it up using iCloud or iTunes—it's your safety net for contacts, photos, app data, and more. This crucial step ensures that even after the reset, your important information will return right alongside your phone's fresh start.

Reasons for a Factory Reset

A factory reset is a comprehensive measure that returns your iPhone to its original state, erasing all data, settings, and personalization. When your iPhone experiences severe software glitches, persistent crashes, or unresponsive behavior despite attempting various troubleshooting steps, a factory reset might resolve these issues.

It's also good to do a factory reset before selling, giving away, or trading in your iPhone, ensuring that your personal data is entirely removed from the device.

Preparing for a Factory Reset

Backing up crucial data using iCloud or iTunes ensures the preservation of vital information like contacts, photos, videos, app data, and settings. This safeguards your ability to restore this data post-reset.

iCloud Backup

1. Go to "Settings" > [Your Name] > "iCloud" > "iCloud Backup" > "Back Up Now."

2. Ensure all desired data is selected for backup, and the process completes successfully.

iTunes Backup

1. Connect your iPhone to a computer with iTunes installed.

2. Select your iPhone in iTunes and click on "Back Up Now."

Sign Out of Accounts

Before initiating the factory reset, sign out of iCloud, iTunes, and any other linked accounts to prevent potential activation locks or issues post-reset.

Sign Out Steps

1. Open "Settings"> [Your Name] > "Sign Out" (for iCloud).

2. Go to "Settings" > [Your Name] > "iTunes & App Store" > Tap on your Apple ID > "Sign Out."

Performing a Factory Reset

1. Open the "Settings" app on your iPhone

2. Navigating to General - Scroll down and tap on "General."

3. Selecting Reset - Scroll to the bottom and choose "Reset."

4. Erase All Content and Settings - Tap on "Erase All Content and Settings."

5. Confirmation - Confirm your decision to proceed with the factory reset. The process might take some time, and the device will reboot, essentially becoming as if it were brand new.

Post-Reset Considerations

After the factory reset, restore your data using the backup created earlier via iCloud or iTunes. Manually reinstall apps and reconfigure settings based on your preferences after the reset.

A factory reset permanently erases all data and settings. Ensure you've backed up all crucial information before proceeding to avoid permanent loss.

Consider a factory reset only after exhausting all other troubleshooting methods. It should be a final step in addressing persistent issues.

If uncertain or encountering difficulties, seek guidance from Apple Support or an experienced individual to ensure a seamless process and avoid potential pitfalls.

A factory reset is a significant step that should be approached with caution. While it can effectively address critical software issues or prepare the device for new ownership, understanding its consequences and meticulously backing up data is crucial before proceeding.

End-Book Review Request Page

Before You Go...

You have the foundation you need in order to keep up with the evolutions of phone technology, and that's going to make the road ahead so much easier. Why not take a moment to help someone else start the same journey?

Simply by sharing your honest opinion of this book and a little about your own experience, you'll show new readers where they can find the help they need to demystify their iPhones.

Thank you so much for your support. It makes a world of difference.

Conclusion

The iPhone is made on a global scale, and it blends computers, the Internet, communications, and artificial intelligence in one blockbuster, game-changing innovation. It reflects so many of the things that our contemporary world is good at - indeed, great at.
—Tyler Cowen

During this journey, you've delved into a transformative experience, discovering the immense potential residing within your iPhone. It's more than a mere device; it's a transformative instrument that elevates your everyday experiences in ways you might not have imagined. As you progress, you should now feel not just empowered, but also confident in harnessing this incredible tool to its maximum capacity.

Our mission has been crystal clear from the start: To demystify technology and to equip you with the knowledge to confidently navigate your iPhone with ease. Let's recap some of the pivotal milestones we've journeyed through together:

1. Grasping the basics: At the onset, we focused on the foundational elements of your iPhone. From the initial setup to navigating through menus, understanding the settings, and getting comfortable with the interface, this stage ensured you were well-versed in the iPhone's primary functionalities.

2. Mastering essential functions: Moving beyond the basics, we homed in on the critical everyday tasks. These included making and receiving calls, sending texts, managing contacts, and mastering touch gestures, making your interaction with the device seamless and efficient.

3. The world of apps: We embarked on an exploration of the App Store, uncovering a myriad of applications. From learning how to download and organize apps, to managing updates and discovering new ones tailored to your interests, this stage broadened the horizons of what your iPhone could accomplish.

4. Connected always: Staying connected with family and friends was a significant focus. We delved into email usage, introduced video calling through FaceTime, and explored social media platforms, ensuring you felt at ease navigating the digital landscape for maintaining meaningful connections.

5. Guarding your privacy: Understanding the ins and outs of iPhone security was paramount. From setting up passcodes and Touch ID to exploring privacy settings and managing app permissions, your digital safety was prioritized.

6. Personalizing your experience: The iPhone isn't one-size-fits-all, so we delved into the accessibility settings. Tailoring features like VoiceOver, larger text options, or screen adjustments ensured your iPhone experience was customized to your specific needs.

7. Capturing and sharing moments: Exploring media applications allowed you to effortlessly organize, edit, and share your photos and videos. From creating albums to sharing memories with loved ones, these apps made capturing and reliving moments a breeze.

8. Smooth sailing: We covered troubleshooting strategies and the importance of staying updated. Learning to address common issues and ensuring your iPhone's software was up-to-date helped maintain a smooth and hassle-free user experience.

Each milestone was designed to empower you, ensuring you feel confident and capable in utilizing your iPhone's diverse capabilities to enrich your life and stay connected in this digital age.

Remember, your learning journey is a perpetual adventure! As you continue to explore and experiment with your iPhone, you'll unveil new features and functionalities. This is the perfect moment to put your knowledge into practice. Apply what you've learned, seek deeper insights, and don't hesitate to share your experiences with those around you. Your newfound expertise isn't just for you—it's a beacon for others navigating their way through iPhone proficiency.

As you continue your journey with the iPhone, don't hesitate to explore further. Dive into new features, discover hidden functionalities, and experiment with different settings. Your iPhone is a treasure trove of capabilities waiting to be explored.

Moreover, share your experiences with friends and family. They might benefit from your insights and discoveries. Your journey is not just about personal growth but also about enriching the experiences of those around you.

And remember, technology evolves, and so does your iPhone. Stay updated with the latest advancements, features, and updates. It's a thrilling ride, and there's always something new on the horizon!

You've unraveled the potential of your iPhone, and there's a world of possibilities awaiting you. Please leave a review as your feedback and insights can be invaluable for others setting out on similar technological journeys. Keep your curiosity alive, your willingness to learn vibrantly, and let your experiences be a guiding light for fellow explorers. Your journey continues, and with each step, you're becoming a seasoned navigator of the digital realm.

References

- *A getting started tour of your iPhone.* (2017). Senior Tech Club. https://seniortechclub.com/tech-recipe/a-getting-started-tour-of-your-iphone/

- *Accessibility support - Official apple support.* (2023). Apple. https://support.apple.com/en-gb/accessibility

- Adams, A. (2022, February 20). *When words become unclear, I shall focus with photographs. When images become inadequate, I shall be content with silence.* PetaPixel. https://petapixel.com/photography-quotes/

- *Adding and finding people in the Contacts App.* (2019). Senior Tech Club. https://seniortechclub.com/tech-recipe/adding-and-finding-people-in-the-contacts-app-recipe-131/

- *Adjust how iPhone responds to your touch.* (2023). Apple Support. https://support.apple.com/en-gb/guide/iphone/iph77bcdd132/ios

- Aguilar, N. (2020, June). *There's a better way to zoom with your iPhone's camera.* Gadget Hacks. https://ios.gadgethacks.com/how-to/theres-better-way-zoom-with-your-iphones-camera-0312986/

- Amanda. (2017, May 18). *Social media etiquette 101 for seniors.* Hearthstone Senior Living. https://www.hearthstoneseniorliving.com/blog/social-media-etiquette-101-seniors/

- Andy. (2020, December 29). *127 mind-blowing phone quotes that will make you rethink.* Getchip.com. https://getchip.com/phone-quotes/

- Apple. (2016a, May 23). *Apple music.* App Store. https://apps.apple.com/us/app/apple-music/id1108187390

- Apple. (2016b, May 26). *Contacts.* App Store. https://apps.apple.com/us/app/contacts/id1069512615

- Apple. (2016c, May 26). *Mail*. App Store. https://apps.apple.com/us/app/mail/id1108187098

- Apple. (2016d, July). *Apple news*. App Store. https://apps.apple.com/us/app/apple-news/id1066498020

- Apple. (2017, April 10). *Fitness*. App Store. https://apps.apple.com/us/app/fitness/id1208224953

- Apple. (2019, October 31). *Use Switch Control to navigate your iPhone, iPad, or iPod touch*. Apple Support. https://support.apple.com/en-us/HT201370

- Apple. (2021a, July 19). *If an app on your iPhone or iPad stops responding, closes unexpectedly, or won't open*. Apple Support. https://support.apple.com/en-us/HT201398

- Apple. (2021b, September 20). *What is the difference between iMessage and SMS/MMS?* Apple Support. https://support.apple.com/en-us/HT207006

- Apple. (2021c, October 5). *Organize and find your photos on your iPhone, iPad, or iPod touch*. Apple Support. https://support.apple.com/en-us/HT207368

- Apple. (2021d, October 25). *Apple Health*. App Store. https://apps.apple.com/us/app/apple-health/id1242545199

- Apple. (2021e, October 25). *Clock*. App Store. https://apps.apple.com/us/app/clock/id1584215688

- Apple. (2021f, October 25). *Phone*. App Store. https://apps.apple.com/us/app/phone/id1146562108

- Apple. (2022a, March 28). *Use a passcode with your iPhone, iPad, or iPod touch*. Apple Support. https://support.apple.com/en-us/HT204060

- Apple. (2022b, June 22). *Use display and text size preferences on your iPhone, iPad, and iPod touch*. Apple Support. https://support.apple.com/en-us/HT207025

- Apple. (2022c, July 8). *Use AssistiveTouch on your iPhone, iPad, or iPod touch*. Apple Support. https://support.apple.com/en-us/HT202658

- Apple. (2022d, September 15). *Learn which size SIM card your iPhone or iPad uses*. Apple Support. https://support.apple.com/en-us/HT202645

- Apple. (2022e, September 30). *Edit Control Centre on your iPhone, iPad and iPod touch.* Apple Support. https://support.apple.com/en-gb/HT211812

- Apple. (2022f, October 24). *Delete photos on your iPhone or iPad.* Apple Support. https://support.apple.com/en-us/HT205856

- Apple. (2022i, November 29). *Use mailboxes to organize email on your iPhone or iPad.* Apple Support. https://support.apple.com/en-us/HT207213

- Apple. (2022j, December 20). *Use camera modes on your iPhone or iPad.* Apple Support. https://support.apple.com/en-us/HT207260

- Apple. (2023a, January 5). *How to set and change alarms on your iPhone.* Apple Support. https://support.apple.com/en-us/HT207512

- Apple. (2023b, January 11). *Block phone numbers, contacts, and emails on your iPhone or iPad.* Apple Support. https://support.apple.com/en-us/HT201229

- Apple. (2023d, February 15). *Remove or switch the SIM card in your iPhone.* Apple Support. https://support.apple.com/en-us/HT201337

- Apple. (2023e, February 23). *How to add and edit widgets on your iPhone.* Apple Support. https://support.apple.com/en-us/HT207122

- Apple. (2023f, March 16). *Restart your iPhone.* Apple Support. https://support.apple.com/en-us/HT201559

- Apple. (2023g, March 23). *Add a payment method to your Apple ID.* Apple Support. https://support.apple.com/en-us/HT201266

- Apple. (2023h, March 23). *Block pop-up ads and windows in Safari.* Apple Support. https://support.apple.com/en-us/HT203987

- Apple. (2023i, September 18). *Set up your iPhone or iPad.* Apple Support. https://support.apple.com/en-us/HT202033

- Apple. (2023j, September 18). *Use FaceTime with your iPhone or iPad.* Apple Support. https://support.apple.com/en-us/HT204380

- Apple. (2023k, September 20). *How to factory reset your iPhone, iPad, or iPod touch.* Apple Support. https://support.apple.com/en-us/HT201274

- Apple. (2023l, September 21). *About Optimized Battery Charging on your iPhone.* Apple Support. https://support.apple.com/en-us/HT210512

- Apple. (2023m, September 21). *Customize headphone audio levels on your iPhone or iPad.* Apple Support. https://support.apple.com/en-us/HT211218

- Apple. (2023n, September 21). *Use Magnifier on your iPhone or iPad.* Apple Support. https://support.apple.com/en-us/HT209517

- Apple. (2023p, September 27). *Set up your iPhone or iPad.* Apple Support. https://support.apple.com/en-gb/HT202033#:~:text=Press%20and%20hold%20the%20device's,Zoom%20from%2

- Apple. (2023q, September 29). *About eSIM on iPhone.* Apple Support. https://support.apple.com/en-gb/HT212780

- Apple. (2023r, October 2). *Use the Health app on your iPhone or iPad.* Apple Support. https://support.apple.com/en-us/HT203037

- Apple. (2023s, October 4). *Use Emergency SOS on your iPhone.* Apple Support. https://support.apple.com/en-us/HT208076

- Apple. (2023t, October 5). *Use made for iPhone hearing devices.* Apple Support. https://support.apple.com/en-gb/HT201466

- Apple. (2023u, October 13). *Use Live Listen with AirPods or Beats.* Apple Support. https://support.apple.com/en-us/HT209082

- Apple. (2023v, November 7). *About iOS 17 Updates.* Apple Support. https://support.apple.com/en-us/HT213781

- Apple. (2023w, November 15). *How to manually update apps on your Apple device.* Apple Support. https://support.apple.com/en-us/HT202180

- Apple. (2023x, November 15). *How to use Shared Albums in Photos on your iPhone, iPad, and Mac.* Apple Support. https://support.apple.com/en-lamr/HT202786

- Apple. (2023y, November 17). *Access Control Centre on your iPhone.* Apple Support. https://support.apple.com/en-gb/HT202769

- Apple. (2023z, November 27). *How to update apps manually on your Apple device.* Apple Support. https://support.apple.com/en-gb/HT202180

- Apple. (2023aa, November 27). *How to update apps manually on your Apple device.* Apple Support. https://support.apple.com/en-gb/HT202180

- *Apple Fitness+.* (2022). Apple. https://www.apple.com/apple-fitness-plus/

- *Apple Fitness+ available to iPhone users in 21 countries starting October 24.* (2022). Apple Newsroom. https://www.apple.com/newsroom/2022/10/apple-fitness-plus-available-to-iphone-users-in-21-countries-starting-october-24/

- *Apple News+.* (2022). Apple. https://www.apple.com/apple-news/

- *Apple provides powerful insights into new areas of health.* (2023). Apple Newsroom. https://www.apple.com/newsroom/2023/06/apple-provides-powerful-insights-into-new-areas-of-health/

- Archambault, M. (2021, December 9). *How to get Siri to automatically read your incoming messages aloud.* Digital Trends. https://www.digitaltrends.com/mobile/how-to-siri-automatically-read-incoming-messages/

- Ava. (2023, October 3). *How to get Siri to read articles and text on iPhone, iPad, and Mac - iGeeksBlog.* IGeeksBlog. https://www.igeeksblog.com/how-to-get-siri-read-emails-articles-webpages-iphone-ipad/

- Bahar, Z. (2021, August 3). *Are free apps safe to use?* NordVPN. https://nordvpn.com/blog/are-free-apps-safe-to-use/

- *Basic touchscreen gestures in Pages on iPhone.* (2023). Apple Support. https://support.apple.com/en-gb/guide/pages-iphone/tan72489b52/ios

- Baterna, Q. (2022, January 24). *10 ways to maintain your iPhone's battery health.* MUO. https://www.makeuseof.com/ways-to-maintain-your-iphones-battery-health/

- Bhonsle, H. (2017, February 24). *Phone Contacts Book - Senior and Elderly Citizens.* App Store. https://apps.apple.com/us/app/phone-contacts-book-senior-and-elderly-citizens/id1207714735

- Bidasaria, G. (2020, February 20). *8 best iCloud tips and tricks to use it like a pro.* Guiding Tech. https://www.guidingtech.com/icloud-tips-tricks/

- Brisbin, S. (2019, July 11). *A timeline of iOS accessibility: It started with 36 seconds.* Macstories. https://www.macstories.net/stories/a-timeline-of-ios-accessibility-it-started-with-36-seconds/

- Brookes, T. (2019, July 9). *How to check and tighten all your iPhone's privacy settings.* How-To Geek. https://www.howtogeek.com/424624/how-to-check-and-tighten-all-your-iphones-privacy-settings/

- *Bucchianeri, E.A. (2019, August 31). You know something is wrong when the government declares opening someone else's mail is a felony but your internet activity is fair game for data collecting. Pinngle Blog.* https://pinngle.me/blog/99-inspiring-cybersecurity-quotes/index.html

- Burton, H. (2023, September 16). *How to manage privacy on per-app basis on iPhone.* CellularNews. https://cellularnews.com/mobile-operating-systems/ios/how-to-manage-privacy-on-per-app-basis-on-iphone-2023/

- Carey, C. (2017, July 6). *How to check your iPhone's battery usage.* iPhonelife. https://www.iphonelife.com/content/these-popular-apps-are-draining-your-iphone-battery-heres-how-to-stop-them

- *Caring for parents, keeping them healthy.* (2008, June 22). WebMD. https://www.webmd.com/healthy-aging/staying-healthy

- Casserly, M. (2019a, February 22). *How to set a passcode on iPhone.* Macworld. https://www.macworld.com/article/673499/how-to-set-a-passcode-on-iphone.html

- Casserly, M. (2019b, March 5). *How to charge an iPhone properly.* Macworld. https://www.macworld.com/article/673519/how-to-charge-an-iphone-properly.html

- Casserly, M. (2019c, December 12). *How to use iPhone gestures.* Macworld. https://www.macworld.com/article/673399/how-to-use-iphone-gestures.html

- *Change security settings in Safari on Mac.* (2023). Apple Support. https://support.apple.com/en-gb/guide/safari/ibrw1074/mac

- *Change the font size on your iPhone, iPad, and iPod touch.* (2023, August 22). Apple Support. https://support.apple.com/en-us/102453

- *Check your voicemail on iPhone.* (2023). Apple Support. https://support.apple.com/en-gb/guide/iphone/iph003dae603/17.0/ios/17.0

- Cook, J. (2023, September 12). *How to download free iPhone user guide/Manuals for iPhone 15.* UltFone. https://www.ultfone.com/iphone-15/iphone-15-manual.html#1

- Cook, T. "Anything Can Change, Because the Smartphone Revolution Is Still in the Early Stages." *A-Z Quotes*, 2014, www.azquotes.com/quotes/topics/smartphones.html.

- Costello, S. (2023). *What is FaceTime?* Lifewire. https://www.lifewire.com/what-is-facetime-2000237

- Cowen, T. (2014). *The iPhone is made on a global scale, and it blends computers, the Internet, communications, and artificial intelligence in one blockbuster, game-changing innovation. It reflects so many of the things that our contemporary world is good at - indeed, great at.* BrainyQuote. https://www.brainyquote.com/quotes/tyler_cowen_630423?src=t_iphone

- *Create shared albums in Photos on iPhone.* (2023). Apple Support. https://support.apple.com/en-gb/guide/iphone/iph3d2676c9/ios

- Curry, D. (2023, May 15). *App Store Data (2023).* Business of Apps. https://www.businessofapps.com/data/app-stores/#Apple%20App%20Store%20Key%20Statistics

- Davies, M. (2022, May 23). Konsyse. https://www.konsyse.com/articles/apple-face-id-advantages-and-disadvantages/

- Diaz, M. (2022, August 10). *Your iPhone's deleted voicemails aren't actually deleted. Here's why and how to delete them for good.* ZDNET. https://www.zdnet.com/article/your-iphones-deleted-voicemails-arent-actually-deleted-heres-why-and-how-to-delete-them-for-good/

- *Dictate text on iPhone.* (2023). Apple Support. https://support.apple.com/en-gb/guide/iphone/iph2c0651d2/ios

- Eckel, E. (2021, June 9). *Apple's Siri: A cheat sheet.* TechRepublic. https://www.techrepublic.com/article/apples-siri-the-smart-persons-guide/

- Edwards, B. (2021, August 22). *How to set up and use "Hey Siri" on iPhone and iPad.* How-To Geek. https://www.howtogeek.com/742121/how-to-set-up-and-use-hey-siri-on-iphone-and-ipad/

- *8 data leak prevention strategies for 2023.* (2023). Upguard. https://www.upguard.com/blog/data-leak-prevention-tips#toc-7

- Eire, G. (2023). *10 silly, sassy, and strange text messages from grandma.* LittleThing. https://littlethings.com/family-and-parenting/grandma-texts/2609861-4

- *Find files on your iPhone or iPad in the Files app.* (2023, November 17). Apple Support. https://support.apple.com/en-us/102570

- *Force restart iPhone.* (2023). Apple Support. https://support.apple.com/en-gb/guide/iphone/iph8903c3ee6/ios

- Gadsden, T. (2022, November 7). *How to use the internet: A guide for older adults.* Allconnect. https://www.allconnect.com/blog/internet-basics-for-seniors

- Gallagher, W. (2023, September 19). *Apple revamps iOS 17 App Store with more personalized recommendations.* AppleInsider. https://appleinsider.com/articles/23/09/19/apple-revamps-ios-17-app-store-with-more-personalized-recommendations

- Gelinas, J. (2019, October 27). *17 new malicious apps discovered on the iOS app store.* Komando. https://www.komando.com/security-privacy/17-dangerous-iphone-apps/608243/

- *Get apps in the App Store on iPhone.* (2023). Apple Support. https://support.apple.com/en-gb/guide/iphone/iphc90580097/ios

- *Get started with accessibility features on iPhone.* (2023a). Apple Support. https://support.apple.com/en-gb/guide/iphone/iph3e2e4367/ios

- *Get started with accessibility features on iPhone.* (2023b). Apple Support. https://support.apple.com/en-za/guide/iphone/iph3e2e4367/ios

- Glamoslija, K. (2021, October 12). *The ultimate internet safety guide for seniors in 2023.* SafetyDetectives. https://www.safetydetectives.com/blog/the-ultimate-internet-safety-guide-for-seniors/

- Goldschmitt, M. (2021, December 12). *Best headphones for iPhone: Lightning, Bluetooth, and more 2022.* iMore. https://www.imore.com/best-headphones-iphone-lightning-bluetooth-and-more

- Gontvnikas, M. (2021, June 25). *The 9 most common security threats to mobile devices in 2021.* Auth0 by Okta Blog. https://auth0.com/blog/the-9-most-common-security-threats-to-mobile-devices-in-2021/

- Grannell, C. (2022, May 18). *Best contact apps for 2023.* Tom's Guide. https://www.tomsguide.com/round-up/best-contact-apps

- Halter, H. (2019, May 16). *Adjust your ringer & alerts with iPhone Volume buttons.* iPhoneLife. https://www.iphonelife.com/content/intro-to-buttons-ports-iphone-x-later

- Helyer, D. (2021, February 2). *Every iPhone camera mode explained.* AppleToolBox. https://appletoolbox.com/every-iphone-camera-mode-explained/

- Hoffman, C. (2017, September 29). *Everything you can do with the Files App on your iPhone or iPad.* How-To Geek. https://www.howtogeek.com/327621/everything-you-can-do-with-the-files-app-on-your-iphone-or-ipad/

- Hoffman, C., & Fedewa, J. (2015, March 14). *How to manage app permissions on iPhone or iPad.* How-To Geek. https://www.howtogeek.com/211623/how-to-manage-app-permissions-on-your-iphone-or-ipad/

- Holland, P. (2023). *iOS 17's best new features: StandBy mode, custom message stickers.* CNET. https://www.cnet.com/tech/mobile/ios-17s-best-new-features-standby-mode-custom-message-stickers/

- Hollington, J. (2023, September 13). *Does the iPhone 15 have a SIM card?* Digital Trends. https://www.digitaltrends.com/mobile/does-the-apple-iphone-15-have-a-sim-card/

- *How to use Siri suggestions on your iPhone and iPad.* (2022, September). Siri User Guide. https://www.siriuserguide.com/how-to-use-siri-suggestions/

- *How websites and apps collect and use your information.* (2021, May 13). Consumer Advice. https://consumer.ftc.gov/articles/how-websites-and-apps-collect-and-use-your-information

- Idowu. (2022, May 2). *11 iPhone settings for senior citizens*. IGeeksBlog. https://www.igeeksblog.com/iphone-settings-for-senior-citizens/#Reduce-UI-motion

- *If your iPhone or iPad is running slow*. (2023, August 23). Apple Support. https://support.apple.com/en-us/102598

- Ikullhem. (2017). *The ultimate guide to Facebook for seniors*. Senior Directory. https://seniordirectory.com/articles/info/the-ultimate-guide-to-facebook-for-seniors

- Instagram Inc. (2010, October 6). *Instagram*. App Store. https://apps.apple.com/us/app/instagram/id389801252

- *iPhone basics for seniors: 7 valuable tips and settings*. (2022, May 30). Seasons Retirement Communities. https://seasonsretirement.com/iphone-basics-for-seniors/

- *iPhone calling*. (2023, March 23). The iPhone FAQ. https://www.iphonefaq.org/archives/iphone-calling

- Ivanova, M. (2022, October 3). *How to create folders on iPhone: An easy way to organize apps*. Setapp. https://setapp.com/how-to/create-folder-iphone

- Jarrett, D. (2023, October 11). *How to free up space on your iPhone*. CellularNews. https://cellularnews.com/mobile-operating-systems/ios/how-to-free-up-space-on-your-iphone/

- Johnson, M. (2023, April 10). *16 big advantages of an iPhone you need to know in 2023*. GeeksChalk. https://geekschalk.com/big-advantages-of-an-iphone/

- Kingsbury, S. (2015, July 12). *How to make iPhone font bigger or smaller*. iPhoneLife. https://www.iphonelife.com/content/tip-day-make-text-bigger-and-easier-read-your-iphone

- Klein, M. (2015, October 26). *26 actually useful things you can do with Siri*. How-To Geek. https://www.howtogeek.com/229308/26-actually-useful-things-you-can-do-with-siri/

- Klosowski, T. (2013, April 9). *How much brightness actually affects your battery life*. Lifehacker. https://lifehacker.com/how-much-brightness-actually-affects-your-battery-life-5994135

- Lachance, C. (2016, May 10). *How to use the Phone app on iPhone.* iMore. https://www.imore.com/how-use-phone-app-iphone

- Lacoma, T. (2020, August 2). *How to add your email account to an iPhone.* Digital Trends. https://www.digitaltrends.com/mobile/how-to-add-your-email-account-to-an-iphone/

- Lantz C. Ht., P. (2010, June 29). *Social Media for Seniors Made Easy: Tips & Tools.* LoveToKnow. https://www.lovetoknow.com/life/aging/senior-social-networking

- *Learn basic gestures to interact with iPhone.* (2023). Apple Support. https://support.apple.com/en-gb/guide/iphone/iph75e97af9b/ios

- Leswing, K. (2019, December 16). *The iPhone decade: How Apple's phone created and destroyed industries and changed the world.* CNBC. https://www.cnbc.com/2019/12/16/apples-iphone-created-industries-and-changed-the-world-this-decade.html

- Lim, D. (2023). *How to download apps from the App Store.* MUO. https://www.makeuseof.com/how-to-download-apps-from-app-store/

- Limer, E. (2020, June 30). *How best to charge your phone, explained by an expert.* Gear Patrol. https://www.gearpatrol.com/tech/a624169/smartphone-lithium-ion-charging-tips/

- Lynch, D. (2017, December 29). *How to search the iPhone App Store: The beginner's Guide!* Payette Forward. https://www.payetteforward.com/how-to-search-iphone-app-store-guide/

- Lyytinen, K. (2017, June 29). *Understanding the real innovation behind the iPhone.* Scientific American. https://www.scientificamerican.com/article/understanding-the-real-innovation-behind-the-iphone/

- Macey, F. (2022, August 24). *Home screen.* The iPhone FAQ. https://www.iphonefaq.org/archives/home-screen

- MacPherson, E. (2008, October 30). *How to move Apps into & out of the iPhone Dock.* iPhoneLife. https://www.iphonelife.com/blog/2440/customizing-menu-bar

- *Mail - Official Apple Support.* (2023). Apple.com. https://support.apple.com/mail

- *Make FaceTime calls on iPhone.* (2023). Apple Support. https://support.apple.com/en-gb/guide/iphone/iph7801d5771/ios

- McCann, J. (2017, December 18). *10 iPhone camera tips and tricks direct from Apple's experts.* TechRadar. https://www.techradar.com/how-to/10-iphone-camera-tips-and-tricks-direct-from-apples-experts

- McElhearn, K. (2022, August 24). *Which is more secure: Face ID, Touch ID, or a passcode?* The Mac Security Blog. https://www.intego.com/mac-security-blog/which-is-more-secure-face-id-touch-id-or-a-passcode/

- Meta Platforms. (2019, February 5). *Facebook.* App Store. https://apps.apple.com/us/app/facebook/id284882215

- Minkov, R. (2023, June 6). *How to make the iPhone easier for seniors and the elderly: 10 simple steps.* PhoneArena. https://www.phonearena.com/news/how-to-make-iphone-easier-for-seniors-elderly-parents-tutorial_id128365

- Mokhonoana, M. (2023). *People who smile while they are alone used to be called insane, until we invented smartphones and social media.* Goodreads. https://www.goodreads.com/quotes/tag/smartphones

- Napolitano, E. (2023, October 4). *iPhone Basics: Intro to buttons & ports on iPhone 8 Plus & Earlier.* CellularNews. https://cellularnews.com/mobile-accessories/iphone-basics-intro-to-buttons-ports-on-iphone-8-plus-earlier/

- Nations, D. (2013). *What is AirDrop and how does it work?* Lifewire. https://www.lifewire.com/what-is-airdrop-how-does-it-work-1994512

- Neagu, C. (2017, November 23). *How to avoid the risks and dangers of downloading free apps and games from the web.* Digital Citizen Romania. https://www.digitalcitizen.life/risks-watch-when-downloading-installing-free-software/

- Palmer, J. (2022, October 25). *iPhone vs. Android: Which is better for you?* Tom's Guide. https://www.tomsguide.com/face-off/iphone-vs-android

- Pathak, K. (2020, July 15). *How to delete photo albums on iPhone, iPad, and Mac.* How-To Geek. https://www.howtogeek.com/679759/how-to-delete-photo-albums-on-iphone-ipad-and-mac/

- Pathak, K. (2023, February 28). *Don't trust your iPhone's passcode to keep your data safe.* Lifehacker. https://lifehacker.com/don-t-trust-your-iphone-s-passcode-to-keep-your-data-sa-1850166806

- Peters, J. (2023, May 19). *The App Store had 1,783,232 apps as of 2022.* The Verge. https://www.theverge.com/2023/5/19/23730302/apple-app-store-transparency-report-2022

- Petrosyan, A. (2021). *Internet usage by age in U.S. 2021.* Statista. https://www.statista.com/statistics/266587/percentage-of-internet-users-by-age-groups-in-the-us/

- Posey, B. (2023). *Apple iOS.* TechTarget. https://www.techtarget.com/searchmobilecomputing/definition/iOS

- Powers, R. (2023). *Smartphones are miracles, and they've turned us into gods. But in one simple respect, they're primitive: you can't slam down the receiver.* Goodreads. https://www.goodreads.com/quotes/tag/smartphones

- PSafe Newsroom. (2022, January 17). *Are your apps leaking data? How to know and what to do.* PSafe Blog. https://www.psafe.com/en/blog/are-your-apps-leaking-data-how-to-know-and-what-to-do/

- *Quickly navigate with gestures.* (2023, October 13). Apple Support. https://support.apple.com/en-us/102388

- *Remove apps from iPhone.* (2023). Apple Support. https://support.apple.com/en-gb/guide/iphone/iph248b543ca/ios

- Roland, J. (2023, September 15). *How to upload photos to social media (Facebook, Twitter, Instagram) on iPhone.* CellularNews. https://cellularnews.com/mobile-operating-systems/ios/how-to-upload-photos-to-social-media-facebook-twitter-instagram-on-iphone/

- Sarasota Bay Club. (2023, September 11). *How seniors can use Siri, Apple's assistant, to make life easier.* Sarasota Bay Club. https://blog.sarasotabayclub.net/how-seniors-can-use-siri-apples-assistant-to-make-life-easier

- Schiltz, R. (2022, November 11). *The 19 best phone apps for seniors (2024).* Senior Safety Advice. https://seniorsafetyadvice.com/best-phone-apps-for-seniors/

- *Self-care in NOT selfish.* (2014). Eleanor Brownn. http://www.eleanorbrownn.com/blog2/self-care-in-not-selfish

- *Send email in Mail on iPhone.* (2023). Apple Support. https://support.apple.com/en-gb/guide/iphone/iph742b6abb1/ios

- *Set a passcode on iPhone.* (2023). Apple Support. https://support.apple.com/en-gb/guide/iphone/iph14a867ae/ios

- *Set up Apple Pay in Wallet on iPhone.* (2023). Apple Support. https://support.apple.com/en-gb/guide/iphone/iph9b7f53382/ios

- *Set up Face ID on iPhone.* (2023). Apple Support. https://support.apple.com/en-gb/guide/iphone/iph6d162927a/ios

- *Set up Messages on iPhone.* (2023a). Apple Support. https://support.apple.com/en-gb/guide/iphone/iph3d039b67/ios

- *Set up Messages on iPhone.* (2023b). Apple Support. https://support.apple.com/en-gb/guide/iphone/iph3d039b67/ios

- *Set up your voicemail on iPhone.* (2023). Apple Support. https://support.apple.com/en-gb/guide/iphone/iph3c99490e/ios

- *Share content in Messages on iPhone.* (2023). Apple Support. https://support.apple.com/en-gb/guide/iphone/iphb66cfeaad/ios

- Shuman, T. (2021, April 15). *How to use Siri: A step-by-step guide for seniors.* SeniorLiving.org. https://www.seniorliving.org/tech/how-to-use-siri/

- Simon, M. (2023, August 28). *USB-C and the iPhone 15: All of your questions answered.* Macworld. https://www.macworld.com/article/2043520/usb-c-iphone-15-faq-cable-speeds-airpods-port-thunderbolt.html

- Slavov, M. (2023, November 14). *Apple iPhone 15 plus.* PhoneArena. https://www.phonearena.com/reviews/apple-iphone-15-plus-review_id5847#unboxing

- Stegner, B. (2018, November 30). *10 useful iPhone tips for seniors.* MUO. https://www.makeuseof.com/tag/iphone-for-seniors-tweaks/

- Stegner, B. (2020, January 8). *What is iOS? Apple's iPhone software explained.* MUO. https://www.makeuseof.com/tag/what-is-ios/

- *Steve Jobs quotes*. (n.d.). BrainyQuote. https://www.brainyquote.com/quotes/steve_jobs_416860?src=t_iphone

- Stouffer, C. (2022). *How to protect personal information online: A simplified guide.* @Norton. https://us.norton.com/blog/how-to/how-to-protect-personal-information-online

- Summerson, C. (2018, April 13). *The best ways to automatically back up the photos on your smartphone.* How-To Geek. https://www.howtogeek.com/348220/the-best-ways-to-automatically-back-up-the-photos-on-your-smartphone/

- Tambini, O. (2021, July). *Best iPhone headphones: The top earbuds and headphones for your Apple device.* TechRadar. https://www.techradar.com/news/best-iphone-headphones

- *Text, call or email a contact in Contacts on Mac.* (2023). Apple Support. https://support.apple.com/en-gb/guide/contacts/adrb66592a53/mac

- *Top 5 challenges for seniors using technology.* (2017). Carevision. https://carevision.com/top-5-challenges-seniors-using-technology-2/

- *Turn on and practice VoiceOver on iPhone.* (2023). Apple Support. https://support.apple.com/en-gb/guide/iphone/iph3e2e415f/ios

- *Turn on and set up iPhone.* (2023). Apple Support. https://support.apple.com/en-gb/guide/iphone/iph1fd7e482f/ios

- *Update iOS on iPhone.* (2023). Apple Support. https://support.apple.com/en-gb/guide/iphone/iph3e504502/ios

- *Use hearing devices with iPhone.* (2023). Apple Support. https://support.apple.com/en-mide/guide/iphone/iph470b1833/ios

- *Use Live Listen with AirPods.* (2023a). Apple Support. https://support.apple.com/en-gb/guide/airpods/dev85c352340/web

- *Use Live Listen with AirPods.* (2023b). Apple Support. https://support.apple.com/en-gb/guide/airpods/dev85c352340/web

- *Use Low Power Mode to reduce power usage on iPhone.* (2023). Apple Support. https://support.apple.com/en-gb/guide/iphone/iphcab9aecd1/ios

- *Use the built-in privacy and security protections of iPhone.* (2023a). Apple Support. https://support.apple.com/en-gb/guide/iphone/iph6e7d349d1/ios

- *Use the built-in privacy and security protections of iPhone.* (2023b). Apple Support. https://support.apple.com/en-za/guide/iphone/iph6e7d349d1/ios

- *Use the side, Home, and other buttons on your iPhone - Apple Support.* (2023, November 15). Apple Support. https://support.apple.com/en-us/105103

- Velasquez, S. (2022, June 13). *The 10 best iPhone tips for complete beginners.* MUO. https://www.makeuseof.com/iphone-tips-for-beginners/

- Veldboom, B. (2021). *How do battery charging cycles work?* BatteriesPlus. https://support.apple.com/en-us/HT201274

- Ver, R. (2017). *If there's another iPhone that's better, that's sad for my old iPhone. but it means we get to use a better one.* BrainyQuote. https://www.brainyquote.com/quotes/roger_ver_847277

- Wagenseil, P. (2020, August 25). *More than 1,200 iPhone apps infected with malware — what you need to know.* Tom's Guide. https://www.tomsguide.com/news/iphone-apps-infected-malware

- *What makes it difficult for some aging adults to use technology?* (2020, July 13). Home Care Assistance of Tucson. https://www.homecareassistancetucson.com/problems-the-elderly-face-when-they-use-technology/

- Whitney, L. (2023, September 14). *Pay with your iPhone: How to set up and use Apple Pay in-store and online.* PCMag UK. https://uk.pcmag.com/personal-finance/36803/pay-with-your-iphone-how-to-set-up-and-use-apple-pay

- Wolfe, B. M. (2021, July 30). *How to save email attachments on iPhone and iPad.* iMore. https://www.imore.com/how-save-email-attachments-mail-iphone-and-ipad

- Wolfe, B. M., & Chan, C. (2021, July 14). *How to use the Music app for iPhone and iPad.* iMore. https://www.imore.com/meet-apple-music-app-iphone-ipad-ipod-touch

- *Workouts for older adults.* (2021, April 19). Apple Fitness+. https://fitness.apple.com/ca/program/workouts-for-older-adults/1562415709

- Young, W. (2023, May 3). *iCloud for seniors: What it is and what it isn't*. The Internet Patrol. https://www.theinternetpatrol.com/icloud-for-seniors-what-it-is-and-what-it-isnt/

- Heggeness, Greta. "24 Quotes About Helping Others." PureWow. Last modified October 12, 2020. https://www.purewow.com/entertainment/quotes-about-helping-others

Made in United States
Orlando, FL
23 November 2024

54341691R00129